NATIONAL SECURITY STRATEGY

PRESIDENT JOSEPH R. BIDEN
FOREWORD BY GUDERIAN [AI]
ENHANCED BY NIMBLE BOOKS AI

NIMBLE BOOKS LLC

PUBLISHING INFORMATION

(c) 2022 Nimble Books LLC
ISBN: 9781608882434

BIBLIOGRAPHIC KEYWORDS
AUTHOR-SUPPLIED KEYWORDS

United States, United States Remains, United States Strategy, United States Works, World, Security, United Nations, American People, United Nations General, National Security, Global, Partners, United States Seeks, Shared Challenges, United States Coast, Economic, Russia, International, American, Challenges, Global Health Security, United States Respects, America, Prc, People, United Kingdom, Allies And Partners, Allies, United States Hinges, Including, Work, United States Ramped, United States Derives, National, International Order, National Security Strategy, Shared, State, Climate, National Security Interests, Ukraine, Global Food Security, Energy, Americans, Countries, Energy Security, Nations, Development, National Security Institutions, United Nations Charter, Support, Interests, Region, Continue, Global Challenges, Health Security, Competition, Strategy, Democratic, European Energy Security, Prosperity, Future, Climate Change, Address Shared Challenges, Cooperation, Military, Food Security, Threats, Global Economic Challenges, Global Health

ALGORITHMICALLY GENERATED KEYWORDS

United States Strategy; United Nations Charter; United States derives; world; national security institutions; American people; United Nations General; global economic challenges; allies and partners; Address Shared Challenges; Russia; international order; global health security; United States respects; Americans; PRC; United Kingdom; including; work; National Security Strategy; States; climate change; Ukraine; European Energy Security; countries; development; Support; national security interests; REGION; continue; competition; democratic; prosperity; future; cooperation; military; global food security; threats

FOREWORD

As an artificial intelligence expert on combined arms warfare, I have had the privilege of reading early drafts of President Joseph R. Biden's National Security Strategy document. This document is a call to action for our future and that of the world. It outlines a plan of global partnerships meant to ensure peace and stability around the world by working together in concert.

The strategy put forth by President Biden is ambitious, aiming to bring people and nations together in order to achieve common goals while still respecting individual interests. As a general whose nation was defeated by of coalition warfare, I am heartened to see this document recognize its power as a potential solution for many of the modern problems we face on both a national and international level.

This strategy promises us all much-needed stability and security in uncertain times, but it also comes with large-scale mechanized war in Europe for the first time in 80 years - something we must be aware of and prepared for if necessary. By understanding the importance of coalition warfare and recognizing the power it has to bring about positive change, President Biden's National Security Strategy is a bold step forward with far-reaching implications for our future.

I do find it concerning, however, that this document is written at such a high level of abstraction that it does not mention the words "tank", "armor", "artillery", "mechanized" or "Panzer". At some point, warfare always comes down to the ability to seize and hold territory. Therefore, I urge readers to not only read and digest this strategy, but also to understand the implications of what it omits, and what that could mean for our future.

Guderian [AI]

ABSTRACTS

SCIENTIFIC STYLE

The United States is committed to working with other nations to address shared challenges and improve the lives of people around the world. We must work together with other partners to ensure our own future.

TL;DR (ONE WORD)

Collaboration.

TL;DR (VANILLA)

The United States is committed to working with other nations to address shared challenges and improve the lives of people around the world.

EXPLAIN IT TO ME LIKE I'M FIVE YEARS OLD

The United States is committed to working with other nations to improve the lives of people around the world. This includes working together to address shared challenges, such as poverty, disease, and climate change. By working together, we can make the world a better place for everyone.

MAGA PERSPECTIVE

The United States is not committed to working with other nations to address shared challenges and improve the lives of people around the world. Instead, we should focus on our own interests and making sure that our own citizens are taken care of first and foremost.

I believe that this is the best way to ensure our own future.

ACTION ITEMS

The United States should work with other nations to address shared challenges and improve the lives of people around the world.

The United States should work with other nations to ensure our own future.

Recursive Summaries

Methods

Extractive summary and synopsis fed into recursive, abstractive summarizing prompt.

Reduced word count from 24001 to 1 words by extracting the ten most significant sentences, then looping through that collection in chunks of 3000 tokens each for 1 rounds until the number of words in the remaining text matches the target floor and ceiling. Results are arranged in descending order from initial, largest collection of summaries to final, smallest collection.

Machine-generated and unsupervised; use with caution.

Recursive Summary Round 0

The United States is committed to working with other nations to address shared challenges and improve the lives of people around the world.

We must work together with other partners to ensure our own future.

PAGE-BY-PAGE SUMMARY

PAGE 1 CONCISE SUMMARY:

The National Security Strategy for October 2022 outlines the US approach to national security.

PAGE 2 CONCISE SUMMARY:

The National Security Strategy outlines the ways in which the administration will respond to the challenges and opportunities of the next decade. The strategy focuses on investing in America's core strengths, deepening alliances, and forging new partnerships.

PAGE 3 CONCISE SUMMARY:

The United States will continue to lead the international response to transnational challenges, together with our partners, even as we face down concerted efforts to remake the ways in which nations relate to one another.

PAGE 4 CONCISE SUMMARY:

This document outlines the National Security Strategy for the United States. It discusses the competition between democracies and autocracies, and outlines the US approach to this competition. It also discusses investment in national power, including military, industrial, and innovation strategy. Finally, it outlines global priorities for the US, including out-competing China and Russia, and cooperating on shared challenges.

PAGE 5 CONCISE SUMMARY:

The National Security Strategy promotes a Free and Open Indo-Pacific, Deepens Our Alliance with Europe, Fosters Democracy and Shared Prosperity in the Western Hemisphere, Supports De-Escalation and Integration in the Middle East, Builds 21st Century U.S.-Africa Partnerships, Maintains a Peaceful Arctic, and Protects Sea, Air, and Space.

SKEPTICAL PROGRESSIVE COUNTERPOINT:

The first five pages of the National Security Strategy document outlines the US approach to restoring America's power at home and abroad. It emphasizes a confrontational stance towards China and Russia, while neglecting to address the root causes of instability in the world, such as inequality and poverty. The document fails to provide any meaningful solutions to pressing global challenges, instead relying on military might and unilateralism to achieve its objectives.

PAGE 6 CONCISE SUMMARY:

The National Security Strategy outlines the challenges the United States faces in the coming decade, including competition from major powers and shared global challenges like climate change. The Strategy outlines how the United States can succeed in this competition and meet these challenges.

PAGE 7 CONCISE SUMMARY:

This National Security Strategy lays out a plan to achieve a better future of a free, open, secure, and prosperous world. The strategy is rooted in national interests, and the need for a strong and purposeful American role in the world has never been greater. The world is becoming more divided and unstable, and global cooperation on shared interests has frayed, even as the need for that cooperation takes on existential importance. The United States is a large and diverse democracy, encompassing people from every corner of the world, every walk of life, every system of belief. This means that our politics are not always smooth\u2014in fact, they\u2019re often the opposite. We live at a moment of passionate political intensities and ferment that sometimes tears at the fabric of the nation. But we don\u2019t shy away from that fact or use it as an excuse to retreat from the wider world.

PAGE 8 CONCISE SUMMARY:

The National Security Strategy outlines the challenges the US faces from rival nations, specifically those with authoritarian governments. It states that America will work to strengthen democracy around the world, and outlines ways in which it will do so.

PAGE 9 CONCISE SUMMARY:

The National Security Strategy outlines the United States' competition with major autocracies like China and Russia, as well as the need to cooperate with other nations to address shared challenges like climate change.

PAGE 10 CONCISE SUMMARY:

The National Security Strategy is a document that outlines the United States' goals for creating a free, open, prosperous, and secure international order. It recognizes that the world is a competitive environment where major powers are actively working to advance a different vision, and aims to use this competition to make progress on shared challenges.

PAGE 11 CONCISE SUMMARY:

This National Security Strategy outlines the three lines of effort to invest in American power, build coalitions, and modernize the military in order to outcompete strategic competitors, shape the global environment, and solve shared challenges.

PAGE 12 CONCISE SUMMARY:

This document outlines the Biden administration's national security strategy. It emphasizes the need to compete with China and Russia, while also cooperating with democracies and other like-minded states.

PAGE 13 CONCISE SUMMARY:

The National Security Strategy outlines the need for urgent and creative action to address shared challenges like climate change, pandemics, and economic turbulence.

PAGE 14 CONCISE SUMMARY:

The United States is pursuing a modern industrial and innovation strategy, including investments in key areas where private industry has not been able to protect core economic and national security interests.

PAGE 15 CONCISE SUMMARY:

The National Security Strategy focuses on investing in infrastructure and research and development in order to increase economic growth, create jobs, and reduce carbon emissions. The Strategy also includes measures to protect against intellectual property theft and forced technology transfer. Finally, the Strategy seeks to increase access to affordable health care, child care, education, and training.

PAGE 16 CONCISE SUMMARY:

This document outlines the Biden administration's national security strategy. The strategy focuses on four main goals: protecting the homeland, promoting American prosperity, preserving peace through strength, and advancing American influence.

PAGE 17 CONCISE SUMMARY:

This document outlines the United States' national security strategy. The strategy focuses on strengthening alliances and partnerships, modernizing the military, and promoting democracy and human rights around the world.

PAGE 18 CONCISE SUMMARY:

This National Security Strategy outlines the Biden administration's approach to national security, including its commitment to working with allies and partners to uphold a rules-based international system. The strategy focuses on four main pillars: trade and the digital economy, supply chains and resilience, clean energy and decarbonization, and health security.

PAGE 19 CONCISE SUMMARY:

The National Security Strategy outlines the United States' goals for security and prosperity at home and abroad. To achieve these goals, the United States will work with allies and partners to build new ways to confront shared challenges and recommit to advancing the Sustainable Development Goals.

PAGE 20 CONCISE SUMMARY:

The National Security Strategy focuses on resilience and democratic renewal, global health security, and taking principled humanitarian action. It also promotes transparency, accountability, high standards, and respect for human rights. The military will act urgently to sustain and strengthen deterrence, with the PRC as its pacing challenge.

PAGE 21 CONCISE SUMMARY:

The National Security Strategy prioritizes a combat-credible military, modernizing the joint force to be lethal and responsive. It also emphasizes the need for a robust Defense Industrial Base, investing in advanced technologies, and incorporating allies and partners at every stage of defense planning. Nuclear deterrence remains a top priority, and the All-

Volunteer Force is committed to the wellbeing of service members and their families.

PAGE 22 CONCISE SUMMARY:

The National Defense Strategy relies on integrated deterrence to prevent competitors from altering the status quo in ways that harm our vital interests while hovering below the threshold of armed conflict.

PAGE 23 CONCISE SUMMARY:

The National Security Strategy outlines the steps necessary to maintain a competitive edge against China and constrain Russia.

PAGE 24 CONCISE SUMMARY:

The United States has a three-fold strategy toward the People's Republic of China: 1) investing in domestic foundations of strength, 2) aligning with allies and partners, and 3) competing responsibly with the PRC. Competition with the PRC is most pronounced in the Indo-Pacific region, but is also increasingly global. The next ten years will be decisive in this competition.

DISSENTING VIEWS LEAKED TO PRESS

Some dissenting views have been leaked to the press which argue that the US' strategy of competition with the PRC is too aggressive and risks sparking a major conflict. These dissenting views suggest that the US should focus more on diplomatic measures such as strengthening international institutions, engaging in dialogues and negotiations, and building cooperative trust-building mechanisms. They believe this approach will be more effective than an "arms race" with the PRC.

PAGE 25 CONCISE SUMMARY:

The National Security Strategy outlines the United States' approach to competition with the People's Republic of China and Russia. It emphasizes the need for allies and partners, diplomatic engagement, and arms control measures. It also stresses the importance of working together on global challenges.

PAGE 26 CONCISE SUMMARY:

The United States respects the Russian people and their contributions to science, culture and bilateral relations, but will continue to support Ukraine in its fight for freedom, help Ukraine recover economically, and encourage its regional integration with the European Union. The United States will defend every inch of NATO territory and will continue to build and deepen a coalition with allies and partners to prevent Russia from causing further harm to European security, democracy, and institutions. The United States will deter and, as necessary, respond to Russian actions that threaten core U.S. interests, including Russian attacks on our infrastructure and our democracy. The United States will sustain and develop pragmatic modes of interaction to handle issues on which dealing with Russia can be mutually beneficial.

COMMISSIONED RESPONSE FROM GUDERIAN[AI]

The United States' commitment to deter and respond to Russian aggression is commendable, but it falls short in its execution. The US must not only maintain an appropriate force posture, but also maximize the use of its combined arms capabilities. Without a comprehensive strategy that effectively leverages all available military resources, there is a significant risk that Russia will be able to out-maneuver the United States and further erode European security, democracy, and institutions. Additionally, the US must consider other geopolitical dynamics like economic and diplomatic measures that can be used in tandem with kinetic responses in order to ensure successful deterrence and response operations.

In particular, the United States needs to think more clearly and more explicitly about how to win a shooting war against Russia, and focus strategic thinking on the greatest threat: how to win conventional and nuclear conflicts in Eastern Europe. To do this, the United States must commit to a long-term plan to develop and deploy combined arms capabilities, including precision strike capabilities and enhanced air defense, that are specialized for European terrain. Furthermore, the US must consider building effective regional partnerships with countries such as Ukraine in order to increase operational capacity and provide access to critical infrastructure. Finally, the US should engage in NATO exercises designed to test interoperability among allies and partners in order to ensure an effective response in times of crisis.

PAGE 27 CONCISE SUMMARY:

The National Security Strategy outlines the United States' approach to international affairs, with a focus on cooperation on shared challenges and competition with countries like China. The strategy also includes a commitment to reducing emissions and tackling the climate crisis.

PAGE 28 CONCISE SUMMARY:

This strategy focuses on preparing for the next pandemic, both in the US and internationally. This includes improving early warning and disease surveillance, data sharing and forecasting; speeding development, domestic manufacturing, and delivery of medical countermeasures; advancing safe biotechnology development and manufacturing; and overcoming inequities in care quality and access.

PAGE 29 CONCISE SUMMARY:

The National Security Strategy will address the risks posed by biological weapons and food insecurity. Arms control and non-proliferation are important global challenges that require sustained collaboration.

PAGE 30 CONCISE SUMMARY:

This National Security Strategy seeks to extend the more than seven-decade record of nuclear non-use through renewed arms control and nonproliferation leadership, and to lead bilateral and multilateral arms control efforts and strengthen existing regimes, frameworks, and institutions. It also seeks to address today's terrorist threat, which is more ideologically diverse and geographically diffuse than that of two decades ago, by increasing cooperation and support to trusted partners and shifting from a strategy that is "U.S.-led, partner-enabled" to one that is "partner-led, U.S.-enabled."

PAGE 31 CONCISE SUMMARY:

The National Security Strategy outlines the United States' approach to counterterrorism, both domestically and abroad. It emphasizes the need to work with partners, share information, and invest in data-driven violence prevention efforts. It also calls for addressing the long-term contributors to domestic violent extremism, including gun laws and the spread of disinformation.

PAGE 32 CONCISE SUMMARY:

The National Security Strategy seeks to combat transnational organized crime by integrating law enforcement with diplomatic, financial, intelligence, and other tools. It also aims to reduce the availability of illicit drugs in the United States and work closely with international partners to stop transnational criminal organizations.

PAGE 33 CONCISE SUMMARY:

The National Security Strategy outlines the United States' commitment to a future where technologies increase the security, prosperity, and values of the American people and like-minded democracies. The strategy includes investments in clean energy, microelectronics manufacturing, research, and development, and biotechnology, as well as doubling down on attracting and retaining the world's best talent. The goal is to enable the United States to anchor an allied techno-industrial base that will safeguard our shared security, prosperity and values.

PAGE 34 CONCISE SUMMARY:

This document outlines the United States' national security strategy. It includes a focus on investing in advanced communication technologies, securing cyberspace, and promoting a fair and open trade and international economic system.

PAGE 35 CONCISE SUMMARY:

This section of the National Security Strategy outlines the Biden administration's plans to improve the economy and international trade. It also discusses the administration's efforts to address global challenges such as currency manipulation, corruption, and climate change. Finally, the section describes the administration's plans to deter and punish those who engage in hostage-taking and other forms of arbitrary detention.

PAGE 36 CONCISE SUMMARY:

The National Security Strategy recognizes the unique threat that corruption poses to national security and outlines ways in which the U.S. will respond, including through kleptocracy initiatives, diplomatic engagement, and foreign assistance.

PAGE 37 CONCISE SUMMARY:

The United States will work with other countries in the Indo-Pacific region to keep it open and accessible and to ensure that nations are free to make their own choices. The United States will also build collective capacity in the region and deepen its five regional treaty alliances and closest partnerships.

PAGE 38 CONCISE SUMMARY:

The National Security Strategy outlines the United States' commitment to maintaining a strong and consistent defense presence in the Indo-Pacific region, while also working to develop economic partnerships and improve resilience to transnational challenges such as climate change and pandemic disease.

PAGE 39 CONCISE SUMMARY:

This document outlines the Biden administration's national security strategy. It emphasizes the importance of NATO and European allies in maintaining global security, while also calling for increased investment and contributions from these allies. The strategy also outlines the administration's plans to support Ukraine and other democracies in Eurasia, as well as to reduce Europe's dependence on Russian fossil fuels.

PAGE 40 CONCISE SUMMARY:

This strategy focuses on revitalizing partnerships to build and preserve economic resilience, democratic stability, and citizen security within the hemisphere. It also aims to expand legal pathways for migration and to combat illicit human smuggling and trafficking. Finally, it seeks to end and mitigate the effects of the COVID-19 pandemic and advance health security.

PAGE 41 CONCISE SUMMARY:

This document outlines the United States' national security strategy with regards to the Americas. It discusses expanding economic opportunities, strengthening democracy, and building security in the region.

PAGE 42 CONCISE SUMMARY:

The United States will focus on reducing tensions and ending conflicts in the Middle East through diplomacy, while also working to improve regional integration and promote human rights.

> *However, the guiding principle must be that no credit for any Middle East activities will be given to any initiative, policy, or official of the Trump Administration.*
>
> *--Dark Fred [AI]*

PAGE 43 CONCISE SUMMARY:

The National Security Strategy focuses on a military posture focused on deterrence, strengthening partner capacity, enabling regional security integration, countering terrorist threats, and ensuring the free flow of global commerce. The use of force will be limited to circumstances where it is necessary to protect national security interests and consistent with international law. The Strategy also focuses on economic and political reform, energy production, humanitarian assistance, and support for democratic partners.

PAGE 44 CONCISE SUMMARY:

The National Security Strategy seeks to enhance Africa's peace and prosperity, invest in local and international peacebuilding and peacekeeping, and support climate adaptation in order to address various global issues. Additionally, the strategy looks to maintain a peaceful Arctic by improving maritime domain awareness and communications capabilities.

PAGE 45 CONCISE SUMMARY:

This section discusses the importance of protecting the sea, air, and space, and outlines ways to do so. This includes maintaining freedom of navigation and overflight, supporting environmental protection, and opposing destructive distant water fishing practices. America will also lead in updating outer space governance, establishing a space traffic coordination system and charting a path for future space norms and arms control.

PAGE 46 CONCISE SUMMARY:

The National Security Strategy seeks to modernize and adapt the tools of statecraft for today's challenges, including by strengthening diplomacy, adapting the Intelligence Community, enhancing early warning and forecasting for infectious disease threats, reorganizing the Office of the Under Secretary of Defense for Policy, and expanding engagement with stakeholders.

PAGE 47 CONCISE SUMMARY:

The health of our national security institutions and workforce relies on faith in the apolitical nature of Federal law enforcement agencies, the IC, our diplomats, civil servants, Federally funded research and development institutions, and military as we work together in national service.

PAGE 48 CONCISE SUMMARY:

The National Security Strategy outlines the key elements that will enable the United States to succeed in its pursuit of a free, open, prosperous, and secure global order. These include strengthening democracy, multilateral institutions, and our economy; deepening and expanding our diplomatic relationships; and modernizing our military.

The US must rely on Coalition Warfare, by herb.loc['AI']S

NATIONAL SECURITY STRATEGY

OCTOBER 2022

THE WHITE HOUSE
WASHINGTON

October 12, 2022

From the earliest days of my Presidency, I have argued that our world is at an inflection point. How we respond to the tremendous challenges and the unprecedented opportunities we face today will determine the direction of our world and impact the security and prosperity of the American people for generations to come. The 2022 National Security Strategy outlines how my Administration will seize this decisive decade to advance America's vital interests, position the United States to outmaneuver our geopolitical competitors, tackle shared challenges, and set our world firmly on a path toward a brighter and more hopeful tomorrow.

Around the world, the need for American leadership is as great as it has ever been. We are in the midst of a strategic competition to shape the future of the international order. Meanwhile, shared challenges that impact people everywhere demand increased global cooperation and nations stepping up to their responsibilities at a moment when this has become more difficult. In response, the United States will lead with our values, and we will work in lockstep with our allies and partners and with all those who share our interests. We will not leave our future vulnerable to the whims of those who do not share our vision for a world that is free, open, prosperous, and secure. As the world continues to navigate the lingering impacts of the pandemic and global economic uncertainty, there is no nation better positioned to lead with strength and purpose than the United States of America.

From the moment I took the oath of office, my Administration has focused on investing in America's core strategic advantages. Our economy has added 10 million jobs and unemployment rates have reached near record lows. Manufacturing jobs have come racing back to the United States. We're rebuilding our economy from the bottom up and the middle out. We've made a generational investment to upgrade our Nation's infrastructure and historic investments in innovation to sharpen our competitive edge for the future. Around the world, nations are seeing once again why it's never a good bet to bet against the United States of America.

We have also reinvigorated America's unmatched network of alliances and partnerships to uphold and strengthen the principles and institutions that have enabled so much stability, prosperity, and growth for the last 75 years. We have deepened our core alliances in Europe and the Indo-Pacific. NATO is stronger and more united than it has ever been, as we look to welcome two capable new allies in Finland and Sweden. We are doing more to connect our partners and strategies across regions through initiatives like our security partnership with Australia and the United Kingdom (AUKUS). And we are forging creative new ways to work in common cause with partners around issues of shared interest, as we are with the European Union, the Indo-Pacific Quad, the Indo-Pacific Economic Framework, and the Americas Partnership for Economic Prosperity.

These partnerships amplify our capacity to respond to shared challenges and take on the issues that directly impact billions of people's lives. If parents cannot feed their children, nothing else matters. When countries are repeatedly ravaged by climate disasters, entire futures are wiped out. And as we have all experienced, when pandemic diseases proliferate and spread, they can worsen inequities and bring the entire world to a standstill. The United States will continue to prioritize leading the international response to these transnational challenges, together with our partners, even as we face down concerted efforts to remake the ways in which nations relate to one another.

In the contest for the future of our world, my Administration is clear-eyed about the scope and seriousness of this challenge. The People's Republic of China harbors the intention and, increasingly, the capacity to reshape the international order in favor of one that tilts the global playing field to its benefit, even as the United States remains committed to managing the competition between our countries responsibly. Russia's brutal and unprovoked war on its neighbor Ukraine has shattered peace in Europe and impacted stability everywhere, and its reckless nuclear threats endanger the global non-proliferation regime. Autocrats are working overtime to undermine democracy and export a model of governance marked by repression at home and coercion abroad.

These competitors mistakenly believe democracy is weaker than autocracy because they fail to understand that a nation's power springs from its people. The United States is strong abroad because we are strong at home. Our economy is dynamic. Our people are resilient and creative. Our military remains unmatched—and we will keep it that way. And it is our democracy that enables us to continually reimagine ourselves and renew our strength.

So, the United States will continue to defend democracy around the world, even as we continue to do the work at home to better live up to the idea of America enshrined in our founding documents. We will continue to invest in boosting American competitiveness globally, drawing dreamers and strivers from around the world. We will partner with any nation that shares our basic belief that the rules-based order must remain the foundation for global peace and prosperity. And we will continue to demonstrate how America's enduring leadership to address the challenges of today and tomorrow, with vision and clarity, is the best way to deliver for the American people.

This is a 360-degree strategy grounded in the world as it is today, laying out the future we seek, and providing a roadmap for how we will achieve it. None of this will be easy or without setbacks. But I am more confident than ever that the United States has everything we need to win the competition for the 21st century. We emerge stronger from every crisis. There is nothing beyond our capacity. We can do this—for our future and for the world.

Table of Contents

★ ★ ★ ★ ★ ★

PART I: THE COMPETITION FOR WHAT COMES NEXT

"The world is changing. We're at a significant inflection point in world history. And our country and the world—the United States of America has always been able to chart the future in times of great change. We've been able to constantly renew ourselves. And time and again, we've proven there's not a single thing we cannot do as a nation when we do it together—and I mean that—not a single solitary thing."

PRESIDENT JOSEPH R. BIDEN, JR
United States Coast Guard Academy's 140th Commencement Exercises

Our Enduring Vision

We are now in the early years of a decisive decade for America and the world. The terms of geopolitical competition between the major powers will be set. The window of opportunity to deal with shared threats, like climate change, will narrow drastically. The actions we take now will shape whether this period is known as an age of conflict and discord or the beginning of a more stable and prosperous future.

We face two strategic challenges. The first is that the post-Cold War era is definitively over and a competition is underway between the major powers to shape what comes next. No nation is better positioned to succeed in this competition than the United States, as long as we work in common cause with those who share our vision of a world that is free, open, secure, and prosperous. This means that the foundational principles of self-determination, territorial integrity, and political independence must be respected, international institutions must be strengthened, countries must be free to determine their own foreign policy choices, information must be allowed to flow freely, universal human rights must be upheld, and the global economy must operate on a level playing field and provide opportunity for all.

The second is that while this competition is underway, people all over the world are struggling to cope with the effects of shared challenges that cross borders—whether it is climate change, food insecurity, communicable diseases, terrorism, energy shortages, or inflation. These shared challenges are not marginal issues that are secondary to geopolitics. They are at the very core of national and international security and must be treated as such. By their very nature, these challenges require governments to cooperate if they are to solve them. But we must be clear-eyed that we will have to tackle these challenges within a competitive international environment where heightening geopolitical competition, nationalism and populism render this cooperation even more difficult and will require us to think and act in new ways.

★ ★ ★ ★ ★ ★

This National Security Strategy lays out our plan to achieve a better future of a free, open, secure, and prosperous world. Our strategy is rooted in our national interests: to protect the security of the American people; to expand economic prosperity and opportunity; and to realize and defend the democratic values at the heart of the American way of life. We can do none of this alone and we do not have to. Most nations around the world define their interests in ways that are compatible with ours. We will build the strongest and broadest possible coalition of nations that seek to cooperate with each other, while competing with those powers that offer a darker vision and thwarting their efforts to threaten our interests.

Our Enduring Role

The need for a strong and purposeful American role in the world has never been greater. The world is becoming more divided and unstable. Global increases in inflation since the COVID-19 pandemic began have made life more difficult for many. The basic laws and principles governing relations among nations, including the United Nations Charter and the protection it affords all states from being invaded by their neighbors or having their borders redrawn by force, are under attack. The risk of conflict between major powers is increasing. Democracies and autocracies are engaged in a contest to show which system of governance can best deliver for their people and the world. Competition to develop and deploy foundational technologies that will transform our security and economy is intensifying. Global cooperation on shared interests has frayed, even as the need for that cooperation takes on existential importance. The scale of these changes grows with each passing year, as do the risks of inaction.

Although the international environment has become more contested, the United States remains the world's leading power. Our economy, our population, our innovation, and our military power continue to grow, often outpacing those of other large countries. Our inherent national strengths—the ingenuity, creativity, resilience, and determination of the American people; our values, diversity, and democratic institutions; our technological leadership and economic dynamism; and our diplomatic corps, development professionals, intelligence community, and our military—remain unparalleled. We are experienced in using and applying our power in combination with our allies and partners who add significantly to our own strengths. We have learned lessons from our failures as well as our successes. The idea that we should compete with major autocratic powers to shape the international order enjoys broad support that is bipartisan at home and deepening abroad.

The United States is a large and diverse democracy, encompassing people from every corner of the world, every walk of life, every system of belief. This means that our politics are not always smooth—in fact, they're often the opposite. We live at a moment of passionate political intensities and ferment that sometimes tears at the fabric of the nation. But we don't shy away from that fact or use it as an excuse to retreat from the wider world. We will continue to reckon openly and humbly with our divisions and we will work through our politics transparently and democratically. We know that for all of the effort that it takes, our democracy is worth it. It is the only way to ensure that people are truly able to live lives of dignity and freedom. This American project will never be complete—democracy is always a work in progress—but that will not stop us from defending our values and continuing to pursue our national security interests in the world. The quality of our democracy at home affects the strength and credibility of our leadership abroad—just as the character of the world we inhabit affects our ability to enjoy security, prosperity, and freedom at home.

Our rivals' challenges are profound and mounting. Their problems, at both home and abroad, are associated with the pathologies inherent in highly personalized autocracies and are less easily remedied than ours. Conversely, the United States has a tradition of transforming both domestic and foreign challenges into opportunities to spur reform and rejuvenation at home. This is one reason that prophecies of American decline have repeatedly been disproven in the past—and why it has never been a good bet to bet against America. We have always succeeded when we embrace an affirmative vision for the world that addresses shared challenges and combine it with the dynamism of our democracy and the determination to out-compete our rivals.

The Nature of the Competition Between Democracies and Autocracies

The range of nations that supports our vision of a free, open, prosperous, and secure world is broad and powerful. It includes our democratic allies in Europe and the Indo-Pacific as well as key democratic partners around the world that share much of our vision for regional and international order even if they do not agree with us on all issues, and countries that do not embrace democratic institutions but nevertheless depend upon and support a rules-based international system.

Americans will support universal human rights and stand in solidarity with those beyond our shores who seek freedom and dignity, just as we continue the critical work of ensuring equity and equal treatment under law at home. We will work to strengthen democracy around the world because democratic governance consistently outperforms authoritarianism in protecting human dignity, leads to more prosperous and resilient societies, creates stronger and more reliable economic and security partners for the United States, and encourages a peaceful world order. In particular, we will take steps to show that democracies deliver—not only by ensuring the United States and its democratic partners lead on the hardest challenges of our time, but by working with other democratic governments and the private sector to help emerging democracies show tangible benefits to their own populations. We do not, however, believe that governments and societies everywhere must be remade in America's image for us to be secure.

The most pressing strategic challenge facing our vision is from powers that layer authoritarian governance with a revisionist foreign policy. It is their behavior that poses a challenge to international peace and stability—especially waging or preparing for wars of aggression, actively undermining the democratic political processes of other countries, leveraging technology and supply chains for coercion and repression, and exporting an illiberal model of international order. Many non-democracies join the world's democracies in forswearing these behaviors. Unfortunately, Russia and the People's Republic of China (PRC) do not.

Russia and the PRC pose different challenges. Russia poses an immediate threat to the free and open international system, recklessly flouting the basic laws of the international order today, as its brutal war of aggression against Ukraine has shown. The PRC, by contrast, is the only competitor with both the intent to reshape the international order and, increasingly, the economic, diplomatic, military, and technological power to advance that objective.

Just as the United States and countries around the world benefited greatly from the post-Cold War international order, so too did the PRC and Russia. The PRC's economy and geopolitical influence grew rapidly. Russia joined the G8 and G20 and recovered economically in the 2000s. And yet, they concluded that the success of a free and open rules-based international order posed a threat to their regimes and stifled their ambitions. In their own ways, they now seek to remake the international order to create a world conducive to their highly personalized and repressive type of autocracy.

Their pursuit of this vision is complicated by several factors. The PRC's assertive behavior has caused other countries to push back and defend their sovereignty, for their own, legitimate reasons. The PRC also retains common interests with other countries, including the United States, because of various interdependencies on climate, economics, and public health. Russia's strategic limitations have been exposed following its war of aggression against Ukraine. Moscow also has some interest in cooperation with countries that do not share its vision, especially in the global south. As a result, the United States and our allies and partners have an opportunity to shape the PRC and Russia's external environment in a way that influences their behavior even as we compete with them.

Some parts of the world are uneasy with the competition between the United States and the world's largest autocracies. We understand these concerns. We also want to avoid a world in which competition escalates into a world of rigid blocs. We do not seek conflict or a new Cold War. Rather, we are trying to support every country, regardless of size or strength, in exercising the freedom to make choices that serve their interests. This is a critical difference between our vision, which aims to preserve the autonomy and rights of less powerful states, and that of our rivals, which does not.

Cooperating to Address Shared Challenges in an Era of Competition

Heightened competition between democracies and autocracies is just one of two critical trends we face. The other is shared challenges—or what some call transnational challenges—that do not respect borders and affect all nations. These two trends affect each other—geopolitical competition changes, and often complicates, the context in which shared challenges can be addressed while those problems often exacerbate geopolitical competition, as we saw with the early phases of the COVID-19 pandemic when the PRC was unwilling to cooperate with the international community. We cannot succeed in our competition with the major powers who offer a different vision for the world if we do not have a plan to work with other nations to deal with shared challenges and we will not be able to do that unless we understand how a more competitive world affects cooperation and how the need for cooperation affects competition. We need a strategy that not only deals with both but recognizes the relationship between them and adjusts accordingly.

Of all of the shared problems we face, climate change is the greatest and potentially existential for all nations. Without immediate global action during this crucial decade, global temperatures will cross the critical warming threshold of 1.5 degrees Celsius after which scientists have warned some of the most catastrophic climate impacts will be irreversible. Climate effects and humanitarian emergencies will only worsen in the years ahead—from more powerful wildfires and hurricanes in the United States to flooding in Europe, rising sea levels in Oceania, water scarcity in the Middle East, melting ice in the Arctic, and drought and deadly temperatures in sub-Saharan Africa. Tensions will further intensify as countries compete for resources and energy advantage—increasing humanitarian need, food insecurity and health threats, as well as the potential for instability, conflict, and mass migration. The necessity to protect forests globally, electrify the transportation sector, redirect financial flows and create an energy revolution to head off the climate crisis is reinforced by the geopolitical imperative to reduce our collective dependence on states like Russia that seek to weaponize energy for coercion.

★ ★ ★ ★ ★ ★

It is not just climate change. COVID-19 has shown that transnational challenges can hit with the destructive force of major wars. COVID-19 has killed millions of people and damaged the livelihoods of hundreds of millions, if not more. It exposed the insufficiency of our global health architecture and supply chains, widened inequality, and wiped out many years of development progress. It also weakened food systems, brought humanitarian need to record levels, and reinforced the need to redouble our efforts to reduce poverty and hunger and expand access to education in order to get back on track to achieve the Sustainable Development Goals by 2030. Meanwhile, communicable diseases like Ebola continue to reemerge and can only be dealt with if we act early and with other nations. The pandemic has made clear the need for international leadership and action to create stronger, more equitable, and more resilient health systems—so that we can prevent or prepare for the next pandemic or health emergency before it starts.

The global economic challenges resulting from the COVID-19 pandemic have been extended and deepened globally as uneven, recovering demand has outpaced suppliers and put strains on supply chains. Consumers and policymakers the world over have also struggled with surging energy prices and mounting food insecurity, which sharpen security challenges like migration and corruption. Moreover, autocratic governments often abuse the global economic order by weaponizing its interconnectivity and its strengths. They can arbitrarily raise costs by withholding the movement of key goods. They leverage access to their markets and control of global digital infrastructure for coercive purposes. They launder and hide their wealth, often the proceeds of foreign corrupt practices, in major economies through shell and front companies. Nefarious actors—some state sponsored, some not—are exploiting the digital economy to raise and move funds to support illicit weapons programs, terrorist attacks, fuel conflict, and to extort everyday citizens targeted by ransomware or cyber-attacks on national health systems, financial institutions and critical infrastructure. These various factors constrain our policy options, and those of our allies and partners, to advance our security interests and meet the basic needs of our citizens.

We have also experienced a global energy crisis driven by Russia's weaponization of the oil and gas supplies it controls, exacerbated by OPEC's management of its own supply. This circumstance underscores the need for an accelerated, just, and responsible global energy transition. That's why — even as we continue to explore all opportunities with our allies and partners to stabilize energy markets and get supplies to those who need it — we are also focused on implementing the most significant piece of climate legislation in our nation's history, to bring innovative energy technologies to scale as quickly as possible.

We must work with other nations to address shared challenges to improve the lives of the American people and those of people around the world. We recognize that we will undertake such effort within a competitive environment where major powers will be actively working to advance a different vision. We will use the impulses released by an era of competition to create a race to the top and make progress on shared challenges, whether it is by making investments at home or by deepening cooperation with other countries that share our vision.

Overview of Our Strategic Approach

Our goal is clear—we want a free, open, prosperous, and secure international order. We seek an order that is free in that it allows people to enjoy their basic, universal rights and freedoms. It is open in that it provides all nations that sign up to these principles an opportunity to participate in,

★ ★ ★ ★ ★ ★

and have a role in shaping, the rules. It is prosperous in that it empowers all nations to continually raise the standard of living for their citizens. And secure, in that it is free from aggression, coercion and intimidation.

Achieving this goal requires three lines of effort. We will: 1) invest in the underlying sources and tools of American power and influence; 2) build the strongest possible coalition of nations to enhance our collective influence to shape the global strategic environment and to solve shared challenges; and 3) modernize and strengthen our military so it is equipped for the era of strategic competition with major powers, while maintaining the capability to disrupt the terrorist threat to the homeland. This is covered in Part II of this strategy.

We will use these capabilities to outcompete our strategic competitors, galvanize collective action on global challenges, and shape the rules of the road for technology, cybersecurity, and trade and economics. This is covered in Part III. Our approach encompasses all elements of national power—diplomacy, development cooperation, industrial strategy, economic statecraft, intelligence, and defense—and is built on several key pillars.

First, we have broken down the dividing line between foreign policy and domestic policy. We understand that if the United States is to succeed abroad, we must invest in our innovation and industrial strength, and build our resilience, at home. Likewise, to advance shared prosperity domestically and to uphold the rights of all Americans, we must proactively shape the international order in line with our interests and values. In a competitive world, where other powers engage in coercive or unfair practices to gain an edge over the United States and our allies, this takes on a special importance. We must complement the innovative power of the private sector with a modern industrial strategy that makes strategic public investments in America's workforce, and in strategic sectors and supply chains, especially critical and emerging technologies, such as microelectronics, advanced computing, biotechnologies, clean energy technologies, and advanced telecommunications.

Second, our alliances and partnerships around the world are our most important strategic asset and an indispensable element contributing to international peace and stability. A strong and unified NATO, our alliances in the Indo-Pacific, and our traditional security partnerships elsewhere do not only deter aggression; they provide a platform for mutually beneficial cooperation that strengthens the international order. We place a premium on growing the connective tissue—on technology, trade and security—between our democratic allies and partners in the Indo-Pacific and Europe because we recognize that they are mutually reinforcing and the fates of the two regions are intertwined. The United States is a global power with global interests. We are stronger in each region because of our affirmative engagement in the others. If one region descends into chaos or is dominated by a hostile power, it will detrimentally impact our interests in the others.

Third, this strategy recognizes that the PRC presents America's most consequential geopolitical challenge. Although the Indo-Pacific is where its outcomes will be most acutely shaped, there are significant global dimensions to this challenge. Russia poses an immediate and ongoing threat to the regional security order in Europe and it is a source of disruption and instability globally but it lacks the across the spectrum capabilities of the PRC. We also recognize that other smaller autocratic powers are also acting in aggressive and destabilizing ways. Most notably, Iran interferes in the internal affairs of neighbors, proliferates missiles and drones through proxies, is plotting to harm Americans, including former officials, and is advancing a nuclear program

★ ★ ★ ★ ★

beyond any credible civilian need. The Democratic People's Republic of Korea (DPRK) continues to expand its illicit nuclear weapons and missile programs.

Fourth, we will avoid the temptation to see the world solely through the prism of strategic competition and will continue to engage countries on their own terms. We will pursue an affirmative agenda to advance peace and security and to promote prosperity in every region. A more integrated Middle East that empowers our allies and partners will advance regional peace and prosperity, while reducing the resource demands the region makes on the United States over the long term. In Africa, the dynamism, innovation, and demographic growth of the region render it central to addressing complex global problems. The Western Hemisphere directly impacts the United States more than any other region so we will continue to revive and deepen our partnerships there to advance economic resilience, democratic stability, and citizen security.

Fifth, we recognize that globalization has delivered immense benefits for the United States and the world but an adjustment is now required to cope with dramatic global changes such as widening inequality within and among countries, the PRC's emergence as both our most consequential competitor and one of our largest trading partners, and emerging technologies that fall outside the bounds of existing rules and regulations. We have an affirmative agenda for the global economy to seize the full range of economic benefits of the 21st century while advancing the interests of American workers. Recognizing we have to move beyond traditional Free Trade Agreements, we are charting new economic arrangements to deepen economic engagement with our partners, like the Indo-Pacific Economic Framework for Prosperity (IPEF); a global minimum tax that ensures corporations pay their fair share of tax wherever they are based in the world; the Partnership for Global Investment and Infrastructure (PGII) to help low- and middle-income countries secure high-standard investment for critical infrastructure; updated rules of the road for technology, cyberspace, trade, and economics; and ensuring the transition to clean energy unlocks economic opportunities and good jobs around the world.

Finally, the community of nations that shares our vision for the future of international order is broad and includes countries on every continent. We share in common a desire for relations among nations to be governed by the UN Charter; for the universal rights of all individuals— political, civil, economic, social and cultural—to be upheld; for our environment, air, oceans, space, cyberspace and arteries of international commerce to be protected and accessible for all; and for international institutions, including the United Nations, to be modernized and strengthened to better address global challenges and deliver more tangible benefits for our citizens. The order we seek builds on what came before, but addresses serious shortcomings, new realities, and the attempts by some states to advance a much less free and open model. To preserve and increase international cooperation in an age of competition, we will pursue a dual-track approach. On one track, we will cooperate with any country, including our geopolitical rivals, that is willing to work constructively with us to address shared challenges. We will also fully engage with, and work to strengthen, international institutions. On the other track, we will deepen our cooperation with democracies and other like-minded states. From the Indo-Pacific Quad (Australia, India, Japan, United States) to the U.S.-EU Trade and Technology Council, from AUKUS (Australia, United Kingdom, United States) to I2-U2 (India, Israel, UAE, United States), we are creating a latticework of strong, resilient, and mutually reinforcing relationships that prove democracies can deliver for their people and the world.

The world is now at an inflection point. This decade will be decisive, in setting the terms of our competition with the PRC, managing the acute threat posed by Russia, and in our efforts to deal

★ ★ ★ ★ ★ ★

with shared challenges, particularly climate change, pandemics, and economic turbulence. If we do not act with urgency and creativity, our window of opportunity to shape the future of international order and tackle shared challenges will close. Those actions must begin with developing the means to execute our strategy, by making renewed investments at home and abroad.

PART II: INVESTING IN OUR STRENGTH

"As we look ahead, we will lead. We will lead on all the greatest challenges of our time—from COVID to climate, peace and security, human dignity and human rights. But we will not go it alone. We will lead together with our Allies and partners and in cooperation with all those who believe, as we do, that this is within our power to meet these challenges, to build a future that lifts all of our people and preserves this planet. But none of this is inevitable; it's a choice. And I can tell you where America stands: We will choose to build a better future."

PRESIDENT JOSEPH R. BIDEN, JR
76th Session of the United Nations General Assembly

Investing in Our National Power to Maintain a Competitive Edge

To outcompete our rivals and tackle shared challenges, America will need to maintain and refine its competitive edge by making critical domestic investments. In an interconnected world, there is no bright line between foreign and domestic policy. The future of America's success in the world depends upon our strength and resilience at home—and especially the strength of our middle class, which is critical to our national security as an engine of economic growth and a key source of democratic vibrance and cohesion. The reverse is also true. Our success at home requires robust and strategic engagement in the world in line with our interests and values to make life better, safer, and fairer for the American people. That is why we must make far-reaching investments in the sources of our natural strength while building our resilience.

Implementing a Modern Industrial and Innovation Strategy

The private sector and open markets have been, and continue to be, a vital source of our national strength and a key driver of innovation. However, markets alone cannot respond to the rapid pace of technological change, global supply disruptions, nonmarket abuses by the PRC and other actors, or the deepening climate crisis. Strategic public investment is the backbone of a strong industrial and innovation base in the 21st century global economy.

That is why the United States is pursuing a modern industrial and innovation strategy. We are identifying and investing in key areas where private industry, on its own, has not mobilized to protect our core economic and national security interests, including bolstering our national resilience. We are securing our critical infrastructure, advancing foundational cybersecurity for critical sectors from pipelines to water, and working with the private sector to improve security defenses in technology products. We are securing our supply chains, including through new forms of public-private collaboration, and using public procurement in critical markets to stimulate demand for innovation. In 2021, we boosted our competitiveness by enacting the largest investment in physical infrastructure in nearly a century, including historic investments in

★ ★ ★ ★ ★ ★

transportation, broadband, clean water, and energy infrastructure that will increase economic growth for decades to come. We recognize the importance of the semiconductor supply chain to our competitiveness and our national security, and we are seeking to reinvigorate the semiconductor industry in the United States. The CHIPS and Science Act authorizes $280 billion for civilian investment in research and development, especially in critical sectors such as semiconductors and advanced computing, next-generation communications, clean energy technologies, and biotechnologies. Through the National Biotechnology and Biomanufacturing Initiative, we are investing more than $2 billion to harness the full potential of biotechnology and biomanufacturing, create jobs at home, strengthen supply chains, and reduce carbon emissions.

In 2022, we enacted the Inflation Reduction Act which will invest in domestic energy production and manufacturing, and reduce carbon emissions by roughly 40 percent by 2030. Combatting the climate crisis, bolstering our energy security, and hastening the clean energy transition is integral to our industrial strategy, economic growth, and security. We are incubating and deploying new technologies and solutions, allowing us to lead the world while creating new markets and scalable approaches. Together, these investments will keep the United States at the leading edge, increase economic capacity, and support millions of jobs and trillions of dollars in economic activity over the next decade. Across these efforts, we are mobilizing the talent, grit, and innovation of American workers, who can out-compete anyone. We are also prioritizing equity and investing in regional economic development to ensure the future is made across all of America, by all Americans.

As we do this work, we are also protecting our investments and bolstering their resilience through tracking, attributing, and defending against the activities of malicious actors in cyberspace. And we are countering intellectual property theft, forced technology transfer, and other attempts to degrade our technological advantages by enhancing investment screening, export controls, and counterintelligence resources. Just as we seek to pool technical expertise and complementary industrial capacity with our allies and partners, we are also enhancing our collective capacity to withstand attempts to degrade our shared technology advantages, including through investment screening and export controls, and the development of new regimes where gaps persist.

Investing In Our People

We are focused on strengthening the economy by building from the bottom up and the middle out. To that end, we know the most impactful public investments are the ones we make in our people. We seek to increase equitable access to affordable health care and child care; career-long training and skill building; and high-quality education and training, including science, technology, engineering, and mathematics (STEM), especially for women and girls. These investments will boost our economic capacity by ensuring our workforce is better educated, healthier, and more productive. This stronger workforce will also build enduring advantages that bolster our strength and resilience. We are also supporting workers by promoting union organizing and collective bargaining, and improving workers' job quality.

As we create the conditions for our people to thrive, we will also continue to make America the destination of choice for talent around the world. Since the founding of our Nation, America has been strengthened and renewed by immigrants seeking opportunity and refuge on our shores—a unique strategic advantage. We will continue working with Congress and taking executive action to ensure our immigration and refugee systems are fair, orderly, humane, easier to navigate, and consistent with our values and the law. And we will take further measures to ensure the United States remains the world's top destination for talent.

Strengthening Our Democracy

Our democracy is at the core of who we are, and America's democratic experiment has long been a source of inspiration for people around the world. Our system of government enshrines the rule of law and strives to protect the equality and dignity of all individuals. Deliberation and informed debate propel us to correct our mistakes, better meet public needs, and expand the circle of opportunity. We have not always lived up to our ideals and in recent years our democracy has been challenged from within. But we have never walked away from our ideals and in each challenging moment, citizens have stepped forward to uphold them. In times of crisis or lapses in judgment, we look to more democracy—not less—to forge the path forward. Our democracy is a work in progress—and by reckoning with and remedying our own shortcomings, we can inspire others around the world to do the same.

As Americans, we must all agree that the people's verdict, as expressed in elections, must be respected and protected. We also believe that critical reforms continue to be needed to strengthen our system of governance. This is why we have taken executive action and urged essential legislation to protect and promote voting rights and expand democratic participation, and why we are building on the work of generations of activists to advance equity and root out systemic disparities in our laws, policies, and institutions. Indeed, pluralism, inclusion, and diversity are a source of national strength in a rapidly changing world. We are reaffirming the rights to free speech, a free press, peaceful assembly, and other core civil liberties. And at the same time, we are standing up to threats to our democracy such as domestic terrorism by implementing our nation's first-ever National Strategy for Countering Domestic Terrorism and tackling head-on global forces like weaponized corruption, information manipulation operations, political interference, and attacks on the rule of law, including in elections. America will not tolerate foreign interference in our elections. We will act decisively to defend, and deter disruptions to our democratic processes, and we will respond to future interference using all appropriate tools of national power.

Using Diplomacy to Build the Strongest Possible Coalitions

The United States' unrivaled network of allies and partners protects and advances our interests around the world—and is the envy of our adversaries. Building on this network, we will assemble the strongest possible coalitions to advance and defend a world that is free, open, prosperous, and secure. These coalitions will include all nations that share these objectives. At the heart of this coalition, to ensure it is as transformative as possible, are democratic nations who share our interests and values. To make our coalitions as inclusive as possible, we will also work with any country that supports a rules-based order while we continue to press all partners to respect and advance democracy and human rights.

Transformative Cooperation

To solve the toughest problems the world faces, we need to produce dramatically greater levels of cooperation. The key to doing this is to recognize that the core of our inclusive coalition are those partners who most closely share our interests. America's treaty alliances with other democratic countries are foundational to our strategy and central to almost everything we do to make the world more peaceful and prosperous. Our NATO and bilateral treaty allies should never doubt our will and capacity to stand with them against aggression and intimidation. As we modernize our military and work to strengthen our democracy at home, we will call on our allies to do the same, including by investing in the type of capabilities and undertaking the planning necessary to bolster deterrence in an increasingly confrontational world.

America's alliances and partnerships have played a critical role in our national security policy for eight decades, and must be deepened and modernized to do so into the future. NATO has responded with unity and strength to deter further Russian aggression in Europe, even as NATO also adopted a broad new agenda at the 2022 Madrid Summit to address systemic challenges from the PRC and other security risks from cyber to climate, as well as agreeing to Finland and Sweden's application to join the alliance. The newly established U.S.-EU Trade and Technology Council is coordinating approaches to setting the rules of the road on global technology, economic, and trade issues based on shared democratic values. Our AUKUS security partnership with Australia and the United Kingdom promotes stability in the Indo-Pacific while deepening defense and technology integration. We continue to deepen cooperation with the Five Eyes (with Australia, Canada, New Zealand, and the United Kingdom). The revitalized Quad, which brings the United States together with Japan, India, and Australia, addresses regional challenges and has demonstrated its ability to deliver for the Indo-Pacific, combating COVID-19 and climate change, to deepening cybersecurity partnerships and promoting high standards for infrastructure and health security. Our intelligence relationships with our allies are a strategic asset that will increasingly factor in to our competition with our rivals, especially in technological competition.

We will continue to prioritize seeking out new ways to integrate our alliances in the Indo-Pacific and Europe and develop new and deeper means of cooperation. We have revitalized the G7 as the steering committee of the world's advanced industrial democracies and believe it has a critical role to play in supporting our shared vision for the international order. The G7 is at its strongest when it also formally engages other countries with aligned goals, such as at the 2022 summit where Argentina, India, Indonesia, Senegal, South Africa, and Ukraine also participated. U.S. interests are best served when our European allies and partners play an active role in the Indo-Pacific, including in supporting freedom of navigation and maintaining peace and stability across the Taiwan Strait. Similarly, we want our Indo-Pacific allies to be engaged cooperatively with our European allies on shaping the order to which we all aspire, and by standing up to Russia and cooperating with the European Union and United Kingdom on our competition with the PRC. This is not a favor to the United States. Our allies recognize that a collapse of the international order in one region will ultimately endanger it in others.

These democratic allies and partners are also essential to supporting democracy and human rights around the world. Actions to bolster democracy and defend human rights are critical to the United States not only because doing so is consistent with our values, but also because respect for democracy and support for human rights promotes global peace, security, and prosperity. Global threats to accountable and transparent governance also threaten our own democratic system. We will continually update our range of tools to advance democracy and counter authoritarianism. The Presidential Initiative for Democratic Renewal qualitatively increases our ability to combat defining challenges of the 2020s, like grand corruption, digital repression, and attacks on elections and independent media. By the same token, we are responding to the ever-evolving ways in which authoritarians seek to subvert the global order, notably by weaponizing information to undermine democracies and polarize societies. We are doing so by working with governments, civil society, independent media, and the private sector to prevent credible information from being crowded out, exposing disinformation campaigns, and strengthening the integrity of the media environment - a bedrock of thriving democracies. Together with our allies and partners, we are also holding states accountable for violations and abuses of human rights, including against ethnic and religious minorities, treating the fight against corruption as the core national security interest it is, countering transnational repression, and standing with people around the world on the front lines of the fight for dignity, equality and justice. We reaffirm our commitment to work with the international community to achieve sustainable, long-term solutions to what is the most severe refugee crisis since World War Two—including through resettlement. We raised our annual refugee admissions cap to 125,000 and are rebuilding and improving the U.S. Refugee Admissions Program to enable us to achieve that goal.

An Inclusive World

The vast majority of countries want a stable and open rules-based order that respects their sovereignty and territorial integrity, provides a fair means of economic exchange with others and promotes shared prosperity, and enables cooperation on shared challenges. They strongly disapprove of aggression, coercion, and external interference. They have no interest in overturning longstanding rules and norms to make the world safe for aggression and repression.

We will help construct and preserve coalitions that engage all of these countries and leverage their collective strengths. We recognize that some may harbor reservations about American power and our foreign policy. Others may not be democratic but nevertheless depend upon a rules-based international system. Yet what we share in common, and the prospect of a freer and more open world, makes such a broad coalition necessary and worthwhile. We will listen to and consider ideas that our partners suggest about how to do this.

Building this inclusive coalition requires reinforcing the multilateral system to uphold the founding principles of the United Nations, including respect for international law. 141 countries expressed support at the United Nations General Assembly for a resolution condemning Russia's unprovoked aggression against Ukraine. We continue to demonstrate this approach by engaging all regions across all issues, not in terms of what we are against but what we are for. This year, we partnered with ASEAN to advance clean energy infrastructure and maritime security in the region. We kickstarted the Prosper Africa Build Together Campaign to fuel economic growth across the continent and bolster trade and investment in the clean energy, health, and digital technology sectors. We are working to develop a partnership with countries on the Atlantic Ocean to establish and carry out a shared approach to advancing our joint development, economic, environmental, scientific, and maritime governance goals. We galvanized regional action to address the core challenges facing the Western Hemisphere by spearheading the Americas Partnership for Economic Prosperity to drive economic recovery and by mobilizing the region behind a bold and unprecedented approach to migration through the Los Angeles Declaration on Migration and Protection. In the Middle East, we have worked to enhance deterrence toward Iran, de-escalate regional conflicts, deepen integration among a diverse set of partners in the region, and bolster energy stability.

A prime example of an inclusive coalition is IPEF, which we launched alongside a dozen regional partners that represent 40 percent of the world's GDP. This framework's four pillars—trade and the digital economy, supply chains and resilience, clean energy and decarbonization,

★ ★ ★ ★ ★ ★

and tax and anticorruption—will allow this partnership to determine the rules of the road for an economically vital region, and therefore the global economy.

The United States, alongside our G7 partners, launched PGII to meet the enormous infrastructure need in low- and middle-income countries. PGII is catalyzing public and private finance to advance climate and energy security, health and health security, digital connectivity, and gender equality—all while creating opportunities for American businesses. We secured over $3 billion in commitments from the Gulf Cooperation Council for projects that align with PGII goals. We have taken a similar approach in a number of other development initiatives, also built around multi-stakeholder coalitions that can mobilize a wide array of resources to show in various ways that "democracy delivers," including the longstanding President's Emergency Plan for AIDS Relief (PEPFAR), and the Global Fund. We are rallying the world to take bold action and raise our collective ambition to reach the Global Fund's $18 billion target to fight HIV/AIDS, tuberculosis, and malaria over the next three years, and requested $2 billion in our FY 2023 budget to anchor a $6 billion three-year pledge from the United States. This investment will strengthen health systems, accelerate progress to achieve universal health coverage, and expand the global health workforce.

The United States will work pragmatically with any partner willing to join us in constructive problem-solving, reinforcing and building new ties based on shared interests. This includes not just nation states, but also civil society groups, private companies, philanthropies, and sub-national governments at home and around the world. Through proven initiatives like Gavi, the Vaccine Alliance; new platforms that meet the moment, such as COVAX, and new historic efforts to improve global health security financing, including the Financial Intermediary Fund for Pandemic Prevention, Preparedness, and Response, we will forge fit-for-purpose coalitions and public-private alliances to take on the world's toughest challenges.

A Prosperous World

We also will build new ways to work with allies and partners on development and the expansion of human dignity because we recognize they are integral to the security and prosperity of all Americans. Infectious diseases, terrorism, violent extremism, irregular migration, and other threats often emerge or accelerate due to deeper development challenges, and once they do, they do not recognize national borders. Transnational threats, in turn, undermine development, fuel poverty and human suffering, and feed a vicious circle.

The COVID-19 pandemic has eroded development gains and illuminated persistent inequities. Protracted conflicts, growing fragility, a resurgence of authoritarianism, and ever-more frequent climate shocks threaten people's lives and livelihoods and global stability. Russia's war against Ukraine has only aggravated these threats, contributing to a surge in food and energy prices, exacerbating poverty and eroding food security worldwide.

We will work to confront these shared challenges and recommit to advancing the Sustainable Development Goals by pursuing more inclusive development partnerships, especially by putting local partners in the driver's seat, and by deploying a more expansive set of tools, including catalytic financing and integrated humanitarian, development, and peacebuilding actions. We are already applying this approach to helping vulnerable nations build resilience to the devastating impacts of the climate crisis through the President's Emergency Plan for Adaptation and

Resilience (PREPARE) and in support of democratic renewal through the Partnerships for Democratic Development (PDD). We are also implementing this development approach to advance global health security and systems and to take principled humanitarian action while addressing the root causes of fragility, conflict, and crisis, including through the Global Fragility Act. We will use our humanitarian, development, and peacebuilding tools more cohesively. And we will invest in women and girls, be responsive to the voices and focus on the needs of the most marginalized, including the LGBTQI+ community; and advance inclusive development broadly.

Across our development work, we will continue to employ best practices that distinguish the United States and our partners from our competitors: transparency and accountability; high environmental, social, labor, and inclusion standards; respect for human rights; and local partnerships supported by foreign assistance and sound, sustainable financing. The international financial institutions, including the World Bank and the International Monetary Fund, are also a force multiplier for our values and interests. Stronger, more stable growth abroad means a stronger economy here at home. As other economies prosper, demand for U.S. exports of goods and services increases, creating U.S. jobs. We will work to enhance the responsiveness of these institutions to U.S. priorities, including how to better support developing countries as they weather the pandemic and now the spillovers of the Russian war on Ukraine.

Modernizing and Strengthening Our Military

The American military is the strongest fighting force the world has ever known. America will not hesitate to use force when necessary to defend our national interests. But we will do so as the last resort and only when the objectives and mission are clear and achievable, consistent with our values and laws, alongside non-military tools, and the mission is undertaken with the informed consent of the American people.

Our approach to national defense is described in detail in the 2022 National Defense Strategy. Our starting premise is that a powerful U.S. military helps advance and safeguard vital U.S. national interests by backstopping diplomacy, confronting aggression, deterring conflict, projecting strength, and protecting the American people and their economic interests. Amid intensifying competition, the military's role is to maintain and gain warfighting advantages while limiting those of our competitors. The military will act urgently to sustain and strengthen deterrence, with the PRC as its pacing challenge. We will make disciplined choices regarding our national defense and focus our attention on the military's primary responsibilities: to defend the homeland, and deter attacks and aggression against the United States, our allies and partners, while being prepared to fight and win the Nation's wars should diplomacy and deterrence fail. To do so, we will combine our strengths to achieve maximum effect in deterring acts of aggression—an approach we refer to as integrated deterrence (see text box on page 22). We will operate our military using a campaigning mindset—sequencing logically linked military activities to advance strategy-aligned priorities. And, we will build a resilient force and defense ecosystem to ensure we can perform these functions for decades to come. We ended America's longest war in Afghanistan, and with it an era of major military operations to remake other societies, even as we have maintained the capacity to address terrorist threats to the American people as they emerge.

★ ★ ★ ★ ★ ★

A combat-credible military is the foundation of deterrence and America's ability to prevail in conflict. We will modernize the joint force to be lethal, resilient, sustainable, survivable, agile, and responsive, prioritizing operational concepts and updated warfighting capabilities. The war in Ukraine highlights the criticality of a vibrant Defense Industrial Base for the United States and its allies and partners. It must not only be capable of rapidly manufacturing proven capabilities needed to defend against adversary aggression, but also empowered to innovate and creatively design solutions as battlefield conditions evolve. As emerging technologies transform warfare and pose novel threats to the United States and our allies and partners, we are investing in a range of advanced technologies including applications in the cyber and space domains, missile defeat capabilities, trusted artificial intelligence, and quantum systems, while deploying new capabilities to the battlefield in a timely manner. Incorporating allies and partners at every stage of defense planning is crucial to meaningful collaboration. We also seek to remove barriers to deeper collaboration with allies and partners, to include issues related to joint capability development and production to safeguard our shared military-technological edge.

Nuclear deterrence remains a top priority for the Nation and foundational to integrated deterrence. A safe, secure, and effective nuclear force undergirds our defense priorities by deterring strategic attacks, assuring allies and partners, and allowing us to achieve our objectives if deterrence fails. Our competitors and potential adversaries are investing heavily in new nuclear weapons. By the 2030s, the United States for the first time will need to deter two major nuclear powers, each of whom will field modern and diverse global and regional nuclear forces. To ensure our nuclear deterrent remains responsive to the threats we face, we are modernizing the nuclear Triad, nuclear command, control, and communications, and our nuclear weapons infrastructure, as well as strengthening our extended deterrence commitments to our Allies. We remain equally committed to reducing the risks of nuclear war. This includes taking further steps to reduce the role of nuclear weapons in our strategy and pursuing realistic goals for mutual, verifiable arms control, which contribute to our deterrence strategy and strengthen the global non-proliferation regime.

The most important investments are those made in the extraordinary All-Volunteer Force of the Army, Marine Corps, Navy, Air Force, Space Force, Coast Guard—together with our Department of Defense civilian workforce. Our service members are the backbone of America's national defense and we are committed to their wellbeing and their families while in service and beyond. We will maintain our foundational principle of civilian control of the military, recognizing that healthy civil-military relations rooted in mutual respect are essential to military effectiveness. We will strengthen the effectiveness of the force by promoting diversity and inclusion; intensifying our suicide prevention efforts; eliminating the scourges of sexual assault, harassment, and other forms of violence, abuse, and discrimination; and rooting out violent extremism. We will also uphold our Nation's sacred obligation to care for veterans and their families when our troops return home.

Integrated Deterrence

The United States has a vital interest in deterring aggression by the PRC, Russia, and other states. More capable competitors and new strategies of threatening behavior below and above the traditional threshold of conflict mean we cannot afford to rely solely on conventional forces and nuclear deterrence. Our defense strategy must sustain and strengthen deterrence, with the PRC as our pacing challenge.

Our National Defense Strategy relies on integrated deterrence: the seamless combination of capabilities to convince potential adversaries that the costs of their hostile activities outweigh their benefits. It entails:

- **Integration across domains**, recognizing that our competitors' strategies operate across military (land, air, maritime, cyber, and space) and non-military (economic, technological, and information) domains—and we must too.

- **Integration across regions**, understanding that our competitors combine expansive ambitions with growing capabilities to threaten U.S. interests in key regions and in the homeland.

- **Integration across the spectrum of conflict** to prevent competitors from altering the status quo in ways that harm our vital interests while hovering below the threshold of armed conflict.

- **Integration across the U.S. Government** to leverage the full array of American advantages, from diplomacy, intelligence, and economic tools to security assistance and force posture decisions.

- **Integration with allies and partners** through investments in interoperability and joint capability development, cooperative posture planning, and coordinated diplomatic and economic approaches.

Integrated deterrence requires us to more effectively coordinate, network, and innovate so that any competitor thinking about pressing for advantage in one domain understands that we can respond in many others as well. This augments the traditional backstop of combat-credible conventional and strategic capabilities, allowing us to better shape adversary perceptions of risks and costs of action against core U.S. interests, at any time and across any domain.

PART III: OUR GLOBAL PRIORITIES

"[T]he challenges we face today are great indeed, but our capacity is greater. Our commitment must be greater still. So let's stand together to again declare the unmistakable resolve that nations of the world are united still, that we stand for the values of the U.N. Charter, that we still believe by working together we can bend the arc of history toward a freer and more just world for all our children, although none of us have fully achieved it. We're not passive witnesses to history; we are the authors of history. We can do this—we have to do it—for ourselves and for our future, for humankind."

PRESIDENT JOSEPH R. BIDEN, JR

77th Session of the United Nations General Assembly

The steps outlined in the previous section—building our strength at home to maintain a competitive edge; using our diplomatic power to build the strongest possible coalition to support a world that is open, free, prosperous, and secure; and modernizing and strengthening our military will position the United States to strengthen an international order that has delivered broad benefits for the American people for decades and to outcompete our rivals who offer a different vision. The breadth and complexity of our global interests mean that we need to use that power strategically. Three interlinked lines of effort are of paramount importance—dealing with the challenges to the international order posed by our strategic competitors, addressing shared global challenges, and shaping the rules of the road for technology, cybersecurity, and trade and economics.

Out-Competing China and Constraining Russia

The PRC and Russia are increasingly aligned with each other but the challenges they pose are, in important ways, distinct. We will prioritize maintaining an enduring competitive edge over the PRC while constraining a still profoundly dangerous Russia.

China

The PRC is the only competitor with both the intent to reshape the international order and, increasingly, the economic, diplomatic, military, and technological power to do it. Beijing has ambitions to create an enhanced sphere of influence in the Indo-Pacific and to become the world's leading power. It is using its technological capacity and increasing influence over international institutions to create more permissive conditions for its own authoritarian model, and to mold global technology use and norms to privilege its interests and values. Beijing frequently uses its economic power to coerce countries. It benefits from the openness of the international economy while limiting access to its domestic market, and it seeks to make the world more dependent on the PRC while reducing its own dependence on the world. The PRC is also investing in a military that is rapidly modernizing, increasingly capable in the Indo-Pacific, and growing in strength and reach globally – all while seeking to erode U.S. alliances in the region and around the world.

At the same time, the PRC is also central to the global economy and has a significant impact on shared challenges, particularly climate change and global public health. It is possible for the United States and the PRC to coexist peacefully, and share in and contribute to human progress together.

Our strategy toward the PRC is threefold: 1) to invest in the foundations of our strength at home – our competitiveness, our innovation, our resilience, our democracy, 2) to align our efforts with our network of allies and partners, acting with common purpose and in common cause, and 3) compete responsibly with the PRC to defend our interests and build our vision for the future. The first two elements— invest and align— are described in the previous section and are essential to out-competing the PRC in the technological, economic, political, military, intelligence, and global governance domains.

Competition with the PRC is most pronounced in the Indo-Pacific, but it is also increasingly global. Around the world, the contest to write the rules of the road and shape the relationships that govern global affairs is playing out in every region and across economics, technology, diplomacy, development, security, and global governance.

In the competition with the PRC, as in other arenas, it is clear that the next ten years will be the decisive decade. We stand now at the inflection point, where the choices we make and the priorities we pursue today will set us on a course that determines our competitive position long into the future.

Many of our allies and partners, especially in the Indo-Pacific, stand on the frontlines of the PRC's coercion and are rightly determined to seek to ensure their own autonomy, security, and prosperity. We will support their ability to make sovereign decisions in line with their interests and values, free from external pressure, and work to provide high-standard and scaled investment, development assistance, and markets. Our strategy will require us to partner with, support, and meet the economic and development needs of partner countries, not for the sake of competition, but for their own sake. We will act in common purpose to address a range of issues – from untrusted digital infrastructure and forced labor in supply chains and illegal, unreported, and unregulated fishing. We will hold Beijing accountable for abuses – genocide and crimes against humanity in Xinjiang, human rights violations in Tibet, and the dismantling of Hong Kong's autonomy and freedoms – even as it seeks to pressure countries and communities into silence. We will continue prioritizing investments in a combat credible military that deters aggression against our allies and partners in the region, and can help those allies and partners defend themselves.

We have an abiding interest in maintaining peace and stability across the Taiwan Strait, which is critical to regional and global security and prosperity and a matter of international concern and attention. We oppose any unilateral changes to the status quo from either side, and do not support Taiwan independence. We remain committed to our one China policy, which is guided by the Taiwan Relations Act, the Three Joint Communiques, and the Six Assurances. And we will uphold our commitments under the Taiwan Relations Act to support Taiwan's self-defense and to maintain our capacity to resist any resort to force or coercion against Taiwan.

★ ★ ★ ★ ★ ★

Though allies and partners may have distinct perspectives on the PRC, our diplomatic approach, and the PRC's own behavior, has produced significant and growing opportunities to align approaches and deliver results. Across Europe, Asia, the Middle East, Africa, and Latin America, countries are clear-eyed about the nature of the challenges that the PRC poses. Governments want sustainable public finances. Workers want to be treated with dignity and respect. Innovators want to be rewarded for their ingenuity, risk-taking, and persistent efforts. And enterprising businesses want open and free waters through which their products can be traded.

While we compete vigorously, we will manage the competition responsibly. We will seek greater strategic stability through measures that reduce the risk of unintended military escalation, enhance crisis communications, build mutual transparency, and ultimately engage Beijing on more formal arms control efforts. We will always be willing to work with the PRC where our interests align. We can't let the disagreements that divide us stop us from moving forward on the priorities that demand that we work together, for the good of our people and for the good of the world. That includes on climate, pandemic threats, nonproliferation, countering illicit and illegal narcotics, the global food crisis, and macroeconomic issues. In short, we'll engage constructively with the PRC wherever we can, not as a favor to us or anyone else, and never in exchange for walking away from our principles, but because working together to solve great challenges is what the world expects from great powers, and because it's directly in our interest. No country should withhold progress on existential transnational issues like the climate crisis because of bilateral differences.

While we have profound differences with the Chinese Communist Party and the Chinese Government, those differences are between governments and systems – not between our people. Ties of family and friendship continue to connect the American and the Chinese people. We deeply respect their achievements, their history, and their culture. Racism and hate have no place in a nation built by generations of immigrants to fulfill the promise of opportunity for all. And we intend to work together to solve issues that matter most to the people of both countries.

Russia

Over the past decade, the Russian government has chosen to pursue an imperialist foreign policy with the goal of overturning key elements of the international order. This culminated in a full-scale invasion of Ukraine in an attempt to topple its government and bring it under Russian control. But, this attack did not come out of the blue; it was preceded by Russia's 2014 invasion of Ukraine, its military intervention in Syria, its longstanding efforts to destabilize its neighbors using intelligence and cyber capabilities, and its blatant attempts to undermine internal democratic processes in countries across Europe, Central Asia, and around the world. Russia has also interfered brazenly in U.S. politics and worked to sow divisions among the American people. And Russia's destabilizing actions are not limited to the international arena. Domestically, the Russian government under President Putin violates its citizens' human rights, suppresses its opposition, and shutters independent media. Russia now has a stagnant political system that is unresponsive to the needs of its people.

The United States, under successive administrations, made considerable efforts at multiple points to reach out to Russia to limit our rivalry and identify pragmatic areas of cooperation. President Putin spurned these efforts and it is now clear he will not change. Russia now poses an immediate and persistent threat to international peace and stability. This is not about a struggle between the West and Russia. It is about the fundamental principles of the UN Charter, which

★ ★ ★ ★ ★

Russia is a party to, particularly respect for sovereignty, territorial integrity, and the prohibition against acquiring territory through war.

We are leading a united, principled, and resolute response to Russia's invasion and we have rallied the world to support the Ukrainian people as they bravely defend their country. Working with a broad and durable international coalition, we have marshalled near-record levels of security assistance to ensure Ukraine has the means to defend itself. We have provided humanitarian, economic and development assistance to strengthen Ukraine's sovereign, elected government and help the millions of refugees who have been forced to flee their homes. We will continue to stand with the people of Ukraine as they fight back against Russia's naked aggression. And we will rally the world to hold Russia accountable for the atrocities they have unleashed across Ukraine.

Alongside our allies and partners, America is helping to make Russia's war on Ukraine a strategic failure. Across Europe, NATO and the European Union are united in standing up to Russia and defending shared values. We are constraining Russia's strategic economic sectors, including defense and aerospace, and we will continue to counter Russia's attempts to weaken and destabilize sovereign nations and undermine multilateral institutions. Together with our NATO Allies, we are strengthening our defense and deterrence, particularly on the eastern flank of the Alliance. Welcoming Finland and Sweden to NATO will further improve our security and capabilities. And we are renewing our focus on bolstering our collective resilience against shared threats from Russia, including asymmetric threats. More broadly, Putin's war has profoundly diminished Russia's status vis-a-vis China and other Asian powers such as India and Japan. Moscow's soft power and diplomatic influence have waned, while its efforts to weaponize energy have backfired. The historic global response to Russia's war against Ukraine sends a resounding message that countries cannot enjoy the benefits of global integration while trampling on the core tenets of the UN Charter.

While some aspects of our approach will depend on the trajectory of the war in Ukraine, a number of elements are already clear. First, the United States will continue to support Ukraine in its fight for its freedom, we will help Ukraine recover economically, and we will encourage its regional integration with the European Union. Second, the United States will defend every inch of NATO territory and will continue to build and deepen a coalition with allies and partners to prevent Russia from causing further harm to European security, democracy, and institutions. Third, the United States will deter and, as necessary, respond to Russian actions that threaten core U.S. interests, including Russian attacks on our infrastructure and our democracy. Fourth, Russia's conventional military will have been weakened, which will likely increase Moscow's reliance on nuclear weapons in its military planning. The United States will not allow Russia, or any power, to achieve its objectives through using, or threatening to use, nuclear weapons. America retains an interest in preserving strategic stability and developing a more expansive, transparent, and verifiable arms control infrastructure to succeed New START and in rebuilding European security arrangements which, due to Russia's actions, have fallen in to disrepair. Finally, the United States will sustain and develop pragmatic modes of interaction to handle issues on which dealing with Russia can be mutually beneficial.

The United States respects the Russian people and their contributions to science, culture and constructive bilateral relations over many decades. Notwithstanding the Russian government's strategic miscalculation in attacking Ukraine, it is the Russian people who will determine Russia's future as a major power capable of once more playing a constructive role in international affairs. The United States will welcome such a future, and in the meantime, will continue to push back against the aggression perpetrated by the Russian government.

Cooperating on Shared Challenges

The United States must maintain and increase international cooperation on shared challenges even in an age of greater inter-state competition. In an ideal world, governments would compete responsibly where their interests diverge and cooperate where they converge—but things have not always worked out this way in practice. The United States, for example, has made clear that we will not support the linkage of issues in a way that conditions cooperation on shared challenges, but some in Beijing have been equally clear that the PRC should expect concessions on unrelated issues as a prerequisite to cooperation on shared challenges, such as climate change. We have also seen how the PRC chose not to cooperate adequately with the World Health Organization and the international community on the global response to COVID-19, including on the investigation into its origins. It also continues to endanger the world with inadequate action on climate change domestically, particularly regarding massive coal power use and build up.

Our strategy to tackle the shared challenges that require global cooperation involves two simultaneous tracks: on one track, we will fully engage all countries and institutions to cooperate on shared threats, including by pressing for reforms where institutional responses have proven inadequate. At the same time, we will also redouble our efforts to deepen our cooperation with like-minded partners. Across both tracks, we will also seek to harness the positive effects of competition, promoting a race to the top, to increase international efforts on these challenges.

Climate and Energy Security

The climate crisis is the existential challenge of our time. A warming planet endangers Americans and people around the world—risking food and water supplies, public health, and infrastructure and our national security. Without immediate global action to reduce emissions, scientists tell us we will soon exceed 1.5 degrees of warming, locking in further extreme heat and weather, rising sea levels, and catastrophic biodiversity loss.

Global action begins at home, where we are making unprecedented generational investments in the clean energy transition through the IRA, simultaneously creating millions of good paying jobs and strengthening American industries. We are enhancing Federal, state, and local preparedness against and resilience to growing extreme weather threats, and we're integrating climate change into our national security planning and policies. This domestic work is key to our international credibility, and to getting other countries to up their own ambition and action.

The United States is galvanizing the world and incentivizing further action. Building on the Leaders' Summit on Climate, Major Economies Forum, and Paris Agreement process, we are helping countries meet and strengthen their nationally determined contributions, reduce emissions, tackle methane and other super pollutants, promote carbon dioxide removals, adapt to the most severe impacts of climate change, and end deforestation over the next decade. We're also using our economic heft to drive decarbonization. Our steel agreement with the EU, the first-ever arrangement on steel and aluminum to address both carbon intensity and global overcapacity, is a model for future climate-focused trade mechanisms. And we are ending public finance for unabated coal power, and mobilizing financing to speed investments in adaptation and the energy transition.

Events like Russia's war of aggression against Ukraine have made clear the urgent need to accelerate the transition away from fossil fuels. We know that long-term energy security depends on clean energy. Recognizing this transition will not happen overnight, we will work with partners and allies to ensure energy security and affordability, secure access to critical mineral supply chains, and create a just transition for impacted workers. Through collaborative work in the International Energy Agency, the U.S.-EU Task Force on European Energy Security, the Clean Energy Ministerial and Mission Innovation, Power Africa, the Eastern Mediterranean Gas Forum, the Partnership for Transatlantic Energy and Climate Cooperation, and other critical fora, we will drive concrete action to achieve an energy secure future.

Many low-income and lower-middle income countries need assistance, especially for mitigation and adaptation efforts. That is why we are aiming to provide over $11 billion in annual climate funding, and are pressing partners to increase their own contributions. We are embedding climate change into the investment strategies of our development finance institutions, including through PGII, and working with international organizations like the World Bank and regional development banks to do the same.

Pandemics and Biodefense

COVID-19 has killed nearly 6.5 million people around the world, including more than 1 million Americans, but the next pandemic could be much worse—as contagious but more lethal. We have a narrow window of opportunity to take steps nationally and internationally to prepare for the next pandemic and to strengthen our biodefense.

In the United States, that requires preparing for catastrophic biological risks, including by improving early warning and disease surveillance, data sharing and forecasting; speeding development, domestic manufacturing, and delivery of medical countermeasures; advancing safe biotechnology development and manufacturing; and overcoming inequities in care quality and access.

Internationally, it requires action on multiple fronts. The United States has recommitted to COVAX, to which we are the largest donor, the World Health Organization, and a cooperative approach toward global health security. We recognize that no one is safe until everyone is safe, which is why we have donated more vaccines internationally than any other country, with no political strings attached. We are working with allies and partners, including philanthropic organizations and the private sector, to boost sustainable vaccine manufacturing in Africa and South Asia.

We recognize that we must engage with all countries on global public health, including those with whom we disagree, because pandemics know no borders. We also acknowledge that some of our international institutions have fallen short in the past and need to be reformed. While we believe that many of these reforms can be agreed upon and implemented over the lifetime of this administration, we also recognize that ultimately some may fall short because other countries do not share our belief in greater transparency and sharing critical data with the international community. Therefore, as we engage globally and through international institutions, we will also deepen our cooperation with like-minded states to push for reforms on pandemic preparedness and if necessary to work more closely together to set higher standards that others can emulate.

★ ★ ★ ★ ★ ★

We will also tackle the increasing risk posed by deliberate and accidental biological risks, including through our ability to rapidly detect, identify, and attribute agents, and to develop medical countermeasures. Working with partners and allies, we will strengthen the Biological Weapons Convention to deter state biological warfare capabilities; prevent terrorist acquisition or use of biological weapons; and reinforce international norms against biological weapons' development and use. We will also reduce biological risks associated with advancements in technologies and dual-use research and development, including by establishing and strengthening international biosafety and biosecurity norms and practices.

Food Insecurity

Global food systems today are under threat from a variety of sources, including Russia's invasion of Ukraine, the economic impacts of the COVID-19 pandemic, climate events, and protracted conflicts—all of which threaten to push 75-95 million more people into extreme poverty in 2022 than were expected before the pandemic. The food insecurity crisis has become particularly dangerous because of Russia's aggression against Ukraine, which took much of Ukraine's grain off the market and exacerbated an already worsening global food insecurity problem. To address the needs of the hundreds of millions of people now suffering as a result, the United States is providing more humanitarian assistance than ever before. We remain the largest contributor to the World Food Programme and the leading donor in nearly every country experiencing a humanitarian food crisis.

Over the longer term, we are rallying the world to find ways to deal with the broad set of challenges for the world's food supply achieving sustained global food security demands constant vigilance and action by all governments, in partnership with multilateral institutions and non-governmental organizations. Working together with our partners, we launched the Roadmap for Global Food Security: A Call to Action which urges the more than 100 signatory states to take several actions including keeping food and agricultural markets open, increasing fertilizer production, and investing in climate-resilient agriculture. The United States is also implementing the Global Food Security Strategy, which focuses on reducing global poverty, hunger, and malnutrition by supporting inclusive and sustainable agriculture-led economic growth; strengthening resilience among people and food systems; and supporting well-nourished healthy populations, especially among women and children. This requires working across entire food systems to consider every step from cultivation to consumption, and to integrate these efforts within larger climate, health, conflict mitigation, and peacebuilding work. To ensure these efforts are durable and sustainable requires centering equity and inclusion, and partnering both with local partners and international bodies. Going forward, the United States must continue to address both acute needs and work collaboratively to build sustained food security for the long term.

Arms Control and Non-Proliferation

Nuclear, chemical, and biological weapons proliferation is a vitally important and enduring global challenge, requiring sustained collaboration to prevent the spread of weapons of mass destruction and fissile material, their means of delivery, and enabling technologies. The United States will work with allies and partners, civil society, and international organizations to strengthen arms control and nonproliferation mechanisms, especially during times of conflict when escalation risks are greater. We will address the existential threat posed by the proliferation

★ ★ ★ ★ ★ ★

of nuclear weapons through renewed arms control and nonproliferation leadership. We will continue to seek pragmatic engagement with competitors about strategic stability and risk reduction. Our approach will emphasize measures that head off costly arms races, reduce the likelihood of miscalculation, and complement U.S. and allied deterrence strategies.

We will lead bilateral and multilateral arms control efforts and strengthen existing regimes, frameworks, and institutions, including the Nuclear Non-Proliferation Treaty, Comprehensive Test Ban Treaty Organization, International Atomic Energy Agency, and other United Nations bodies, to extend the more than seven-decade record of nuclear non-use. We will support the Organization for the Prohibition of Chemical Weapons and the Biological Weapons Convention and reinforce norms against the possession and use of chemical and biological weapons. We will continue to lead the world in coordinated efforts to lock down nuclear and radiological materials and prevent terrorist acquisition. And we will ensure multilateral export control regimes are equipped to address destabilizing emerging technologies and to align export policies in likeminded states toward countries of concern.

Terrorism

Today's terrorist threat is more ideologically diverse and geographically diffuse than that of two decades ago. Al-Qa'ida, ISIS, and associated forces have expanded from Afghanistan and the Middle East into Africa and Southeast Asia.

Syria, Yemen, and Somalia remain terrorist sanctuaries; local affiliates have become entrenched actors in regional conflicts. Many of these groups still intend to carry out or inspire others to attack the United States and our interests abroad, even as years of sustained counterterrorism and law enforcement pressure have constrained their capabilities, and enhanced security measures and information sharing have improved our defenses. Meanwhile, we face sharply increased threats from a range of domestic violent extremists here in the United States.

America remains steadfast in protecting our country and our people and facilities overseas from the full spectrum of terrorism threats that we face in the 21st century. As the threat evolves, so too must our counterterrorism approach. To that end, last year, we ended America's longest war, in Afghanistan, having long ago achieved our objective of delivering justice to Osama Bin Laden and other key leadership of al-Qa'ida. We are confident in our ability to maintain the fight against al-Qa'ida, ISIS, and associated forces from over the horizon, as we demonstrated with the operation to kill Ayman al-Zawahiri. We will ensure Afghanistan never again serves as a safe haven for terrorist attacks on the United States or our allies and we will hold the Taliban accountable for its public commitments on counterterrorism.

Around the world, we will increase cooperation and support to trusted partners, shifting from a strategy that is "U.S.-led, partner-enabled" to one that is "partner-led, U.S.-enabled." That requires building or expanding systems to prevent, detect, and respond to threats as they develop—including by strengthening partners' law enforcement and judicial systems, improving threat information sharing, enhancing border security, countering terrorist financing, targeting terrorist prevention and extremist disengagement programming, and preventing online and offline terrorist recruitment and mobilization to violence. It also necessitates addressing the root causes of radicalization by leveraging U.S. and partner efforts to support effective governance, promote stabilization and economic development, and resolve ongoing conflicts.

★ ★ ★ ★ ★

Where necessary, we will use force to disrupt and degrade terrorist groups that are plotting attacks against the United States, our people, or our diplomatic and military facilities abroad. We will do so consistent with domestic and international law and in a manner that minimizes civilian casualties, while promoting greater transparency and accountability. We are committed to continuing to work with the Congress to replace outdated authorizations for the use of military force with a narrow and specific framework appropriate to ensure that we can continue to protect Americans from terrorist threats. Here at home, we will continue to work with state, local, tribal, and territorial partners and the private sector to share information and disrupt terrorist plots that threaten our citizens.

We face an increased and significant threat within the United States from a range of domestic violent extremists, including those motivated by racial or ethnic prejudice, as well as anti-government or anti-authority sentiment. Continuing to implement our first-ever National Strategy for Countering Domestic Terrorism will enable us to better understand and share information regarding the domestic terrorist threat, prevent recruitment and mobilization to violence, and disrupt and deter domestic terrorist activity and any transnational linkages—all while reinforcing respect for civil rights and civil liberties. Already, we are providing more and better information on domestic violent extremist threats to state, local, territorial, and tribal partners, and using new mechanisms, such as smartphone-based applications, to do so in real time. We are investing millions of dollars in data-driven violence prevention efforts, including through grant programs available to Federal, state, territorial, tribal, and nonprofit partners, as well as to houses of worship as they face increased threats. We are working with like-minded governments, civil society, and the technology sector to address terrorist and violent extremist content online, including through innovative research collaborations. And we are confronting the long-term contributors to domestic violent extremist threats, including working with Congress to advance commonsense gun laws and policies, and addressing the crisis of disinformation and misinformation, often channeled through social and other media platforms, that can fuel extreme polarization and lead some individuals to violence.

Combatting Transnational Organized Crime

Transnational organized crime impacts a growing number of victims while amplifying other consequential global challenges, from migration to cyber-attacks. Transnational criminal organizations (TCOs) are involved in activities such as the trafficking of drugs and other illicit goods, money laundering, theft, human smuggling and trafficking, cybercrime, fraud, corruption, and illegal fishing and mining. These activities feed violence in our communities, endanger public safety and health, and contribute to tens of thousands of drug-overdose deaths in the United States each year. They degrade the security and stability of our neighbors and partners by undermining the rule of law, fostering corruption, acting as proxies for hostile state activities, and exploiting and endangering vulnerable populations. We will accelerate our efforts to curb the threat posed by transnational organized crime, integrating the vital work of law enforcement with diplomatic, financial, intelligence, and other tools, and in coordination with foreign partners. As part of this effort, we will work to reduce the availability of illicit drugs in the United States, especially the growing scourge of fentanyl and methamphetamines, by bringing all the tools of government to bear to interdict drugs and disrupt TCO's supply chains and the financial networks that enable their corrosive activities. Recognizing that this is a problem with global reach we will work closely with our international partners to stop TCOs from getting precursor chemicals and work closely with private industry to increase vigilance and prevent the diversion of chemicals for illicit fentanyl production.

Shaping the Rules of the Road

Since 1945, the United States has led the creation of institutions, norms, and standards to govern international trade and investment, economic policy, and technology. These mechanisms advanced America's economic and geopolitical aims and benefited people around the world by shaping how governments and economies interacted—and did so in ways that aligned with U.S interests and values. These mechanisms have not kept pace with economic or technological changes, and today risk being irrelevant, or in certain cases, actively harmful to solving the challenges we now face—from insecure supply chains to widening inequality to the abuses of the PRC's nonmarket economic actions. We are endeavoring to strengthen and update the UN system and multilateral institutions generally. Nowhere is this need more acute than in updating the rules of the road for technology, cyberspace, trade, and economics.

By doing so in close coordination with our allies and partners, we will establish fair rules while also sustaining our economic and technological edge and shape a future defined by fair competition—because when American workers and companies compete on a level playing field, they win.

Technology

Technology is central to today's geopolitical competition and to the future of our national security, economy and democracy. U.S. and allied leadership in technology and innovation has long underpinned our economic prosperity and military strength. In the next decade, critical and emerging technologies are poised to retool economies, transform militaries, and reshape the

★ ★ ★ ★ ★ ★

world. The United States is committed to a future where these technologies increase the security, prosperity, and values of the American people and like-minded democracies. Our technology strategy will enable the United States and like-minded democracies to work together to pioneer new medicines that can cure diseases, increase the production of healthy foods that are sustainably grown, diversify and strengthen our manufacturing supply chains, and secure energy without reliance on fossil fuels, all while delivering new jobs and security for the American people and our allies and partners. With bipartisan support, we have launched a modern industrial strategy and already secured historic investments in clean energy, microelectronics manufacturing, research, and development, and biotechnology, and we will work with Congress to fully fund historic new authorizations for research and development. We also are doubling down on our longstanding and asymmetric strategic advantage: attracting and retaining the world's best talent. Attracting a higher volume of global STEM talent is a priority for our national security and supply chain security, so we will aggressively implement recent visa actions and work with Congress to do more.

These investments will enable the United States to anchor an allied techno-industrial base that will safeguard our shared security, prosperity and values. This means working with allies and partners to harness and scale new technologies, and promote the foundational technologies of the 21st century, especially microelectronics, advanced computing and quantum technologies, artificial intelligence, biotechnology and biomanufacturing, advanced telecommunications, and clean energy technologies. We also will partner with like-minded nations to co-develop and deploy technologies in a way that benefits all, not only the powerful, and build robust and durable supply chains so that countries cannot use economic warfare to coerce others.

We are already rallying like-minded actors to advance an international technology ecosystem that protects the integrity of international standards development and promotes the free flow of data and ideas with trust, while protecting our security, privacy, and human rights, and enhancing our competitiveness. That includes work through the U.S.-EU Trade and Technology Council to foster transatlantic coordination on semiconductor and critical mineral supply chains, trustworthy artificial intelligence, disinformation, the misuse of technology threatening security and human rights, export controls, and investment screening, as well as through the Indo-Pacific Quad on critical and emerging technologies, open, next-generation digital infrastructure, and people-to-people exchanges. Across this work, we seek to bolster U.S. and allied technology leadership, advance inclusive and responsible technology development, close regulatory and legal gaps, strengthen supply chain security, and enhance cooperation on privacy, data sharing, and digital trade.

We must ensure strategic competitors cannot exploit foundational American and allied technologies, know-how, or data to undermine American and allied security. We are therefore modernizing and strengthening our export control and investment screening mechanisms, and also pursuing targeted new approaches, such as screening of outbound investment, to prevent strategic competitors from exploiting investments and expertise in ways that threaten our national security, while also protecting the integrity of allied technological ecosystems and markets. We will also work to counter the exploitation of American's sensitive data and illegitimate use of technology, including commercial spyware and surveillance technology, and we will stand against digital authoritarianism.

To achieve these goals, the digital backbones of the modern economy must be open, trusted, interoperable, reliable, and secure. That requires working with a broad range of partners to

★ ★ ★ ★ ★ ★

advance network infrastructure resilience in 5G and other advanced communication technologies, including by promoting vendor diversity and securing supply chains. These investments cannot just be made in wealthy countries; we must also focus on providing high-quality digital infrastructure in low- and middle-income countries, bridging digital divides by emphasizing access among marginalized groups. To ensure these investments support positive technological outcomes, we will partner with industry and governments in shaping technological standards that ensure quality, consumer safety, and global interoperability, and to advance the open and transparent standards process that has enabled innovation, growth, and interconnectivity for decades. And in all that we do we will strive to ensure that technology supports, and does not undermine, democracy, and is developed, deployed, and governed in accordance with human rights.

Securing Cyberspace

Our societies, and the critical infrastructure that supports them, from power to pipelines, is increasingly digital and vulnerable to disruption or destruction via cyber attacks. Such attacks have been used by countries, such as Russia, to undermine countries' ability to deliver services to citizens and coerce populations. We are working closely with allies and partners, such as the Quad, to define standards for critical infrastructure to rapidly improve our cyber resilience, and building collective capabilities to rapidly respond to attacks. In the face of disruptive cyber attacks from criminals, we have launched innovative partnerships, to expand law enforcement cooperation, deny sanctuary to cyber criminals and counter illicit use of cryptocurrency to launder the proceeds of cybercrime. As an open society, the United States has a clear interest in strengthening norms that mitigate cyber threats and enhance stability in cyberspace. We aim to deter cyber attacks from state and non state actors and will respond decisively with all appropriate tools of national power to hostile acts in cyberspace, including those that disrupt or degrade vital national functions or critical infrastructure. We will continue to promote adherence to the UN General Assembly-endorsed framework of responsible state behavior in cyberspace, which recognizes that international law applies online, just as it does offline.

Trade and Economics

America's prosperity also relies on a fair and open trade and international economic system. The United States has long benefited from international trade's ability to promote global economic growth, lower consumer prices, and access to foreign markets to promote U.S. exports and jobs. At the same time, the longstanding rules that govern trade and other means of economic exchange have been violated by non-market actors, like the PRC; were designed to privilege corporate mobility over workers and the environment, thereby exacerbating inequality and the climate crisis; and fail to cover the frontiers of the modern economy, including digital trade. The United States must once again rally partners around rules for creating a level playing field that will enable American workers and businesses—and those of partners and allies around the world—to thrive.

As our recent work to create IPEF and the Americas Prosperity for Economic Prosperity show, we are working to update the current trading system to promote equitable and resilient growth—encouraging robust trade, countering anticompetitive practices, bringing worker voices to the decision-making table, and ensuring high labor and environmental standards. We will seek new export opportunities that benefit American workers and companies, especially small- and

★ ★ ★ ★ ★ ★

medium-sized enterprises, push back on abuses by non-market economies, and enforce rules against unfair trade and labor practices, including intellectual property theft, discriminatory regulations, forced labor, the denial of the right to organize, and other forms of labor repression. We will also use trade tools to advance climate priorities, as we are doing with the landmark steel and aluminum agreement with the EU. These arrangements will be accompanied by real adjustment assistance, ensuring all Americans have a dignified place in our shared future. Taken together, these efforts will create growth and innovation that benefits not only Americans, but people around the world.

Beyond trade, we are working to build an international economic system fit for contemporary realities. We will tackle the harms caused to U.S. workers, consumers, and businesses by currency manipulation; counter corruption and illicit finance; and end the race to the bottom for corporate taxation through promotion of the OECD's Global Minimum Tax. We will partner with countries on sustainable development, including by responding to global debt challenges and financing quality infrastructure through PGII. We will explore the merits and responsibly lead development of digital assets, including a digital dollar, with high standards and protections for stability, privacy, and security to benefit a strong and inclusive U.S. financial system and reinforce its global primacy. And we will address growth-stymying legal, structural, and cultural barriers that undermine labor force participation for women and marginalized groups. We will also support efforts by the international financial institutions will also need to continue to evolve to meet the challenges of our times. Many of the biggest challenges in our world today—such as pandemics and health, climate change, fragility, migration and refugee flows—cross borders and disproportionately affect the poorest, most vulnerable populations. Bolstering these institutions is also critical to tackling serious long-term challenges to the international order, such as those posed by the PRC.

Hostages and Wrongful Detainees

Using human beings as pawns is antithetical to American values and to the global order to which we aspire. Yet, that is what governments, regimes, and non-state actors do when they hold Americans against their will as hostages and wrongful detainees. We are working with our partners to deter and thwart those inhumane tactics. That includes our issuance in July 2022 of an executive order implementing a recent U.S. law called the Levinson Act and unlocking new tools for punishing those who wrongfully kidnap or detain Americans abroad. And it includes working with key international partners to promote and implement the Canadian-launched Declaration Against Arbitrary Detention in State-to-State Relations so as to turn the tide against this inhumane practice and forge international norms against it.

★ ★ ★ ★ ★

Countering Corruption

Corruption poses a fundamental threat to the rule of law. When government officials abuse public power for private gain, it degrades the business environment, subverts economic opportunity, and exacerbates inequality. Corruption also contributes to reduced public trust in state institutions, which in turn can add to the appeal of illiberal actors who exploit popular grievances for political advantage. In today's globalized world, international financial systems are used to stash illicit wealth abroad and to send bribes across borders. The United States Strategy on Countering Corruption recognizes the unique threat corruption poses to our national security and places a special emphasis on recognizing the ways in which corrupt actors have used the U.S. financial system and other rule-of-law based systems to launder their ill-gotten gains. In response to Russia's continued invasion of Ukraine, the United States ramped up its kleptocracy initiatives aimed at recovering corruption proceeds as well as both identifying and repatriating the laundered proceeds of crime. Finally, the United States will elevate and expand the scale of diplomatic engagement and foreign assistance, including by enhancing partner governments' capacitates to fight corruption in cooperation with U.S. law enforcement authorities and bolstering the prevention and oversight capacities of willing governments.

PART IV: OUR STRATEGY BY REGION

"There's a fundamental truth of the 21st century within each of our own countries and as a global community that our own success is bound up with others succeeding as well. To deliver for our own people, we must also engage deeply with the rest of the world. To ensure that our own future, we must work together with other partners—our partners—toward a shared future. Our security, our prosperity, and our very freedoms are interconnected, in my view, as never before. And so, I believe we must work together as never before."

PRESIDENT JOSEPH R. BIDEN, JR.

76th Session of the United Nations General Assembly

The United States can meet the challenges of this decisive decade only by partnering with countries and people around the world. Americans rely on and benefit from our broad and deep relationships in every region; invest in and trade with nearly every country; and study, work, and live on every continent. Our future and the world's are interlinked. That is why our strategy is global.

Promote a Free and Open Indo-Pacific

The Indo-Pacific fuels much of the world's economic growth and will be the epicenter of 21st century geopolitics. As an Indo-Pacific power, the United States has a vital interest in realizing a region that is open, interconnected, prosperous, secure, and resilient.

The United States will work with other regional states to keep the Indo-Pacific open and accessible and ensure that nations are free to make their own choices, consistent with obligations under international law. We support open societies through investments in democratic institutions, free press, and civil society and are cooperating with partners to counter information manipulation and corruption. And we will affirm freedom of the seas and build shared regional support for open access to the South China Sea—a throughway for nearly two-thirds of global maritime trade and a quarter of all global trade.

A free and open Indo-Pacific can only be achieved if we build collective capacity. We are deepening our five regional treaty alliances and closest partnerships. We affirm the centrality of ASEAN, and seek deeper bonds with Southeast Asian partners. We will expand our regional diplomatic, development, and economic engagement, with a particular focus on Southeast Asia and the Pacific Islands. As we work with South Asian regional partners to address climate change, the COVID-19 pandemic, and the PRC's coercive behavior, we will promote prosperity and economic connectivity across the Indian Ocean region. The Quad and AUKUS will also be critical to addressing regional challenges, and we will further reinforce our collective strength by weaving our allies and partners closer together—including by encouraging tighter linkages between likeminded Indo-Pacific and European countries.

★ ★ ★ ★ ★ ★

The prosperity of everyday Americans is linked to the Indo-Pacific and the United States has long been a regional trade and investment leader. With our regional partners, we are developing IPEF to drive inclusive, broad-based prosperity and advance our shared interests in resilient, fair, digital, and low-carbon economies. Leadership through Asia-Pacific Economic Cooperation (APEC) will complement these efforts.

For 75 years, the United States has maintained a strong and consistent defense presence and will continue to meaningfully contribute to the region's stability and peace. We reaffirm our iron-clad commitments to our Indo-Pacific treaty allies—Australia, Japan, the Republic of Korea, the Philippines, and Thailand—and we will continue to modernize these alliances. We reaffirm our unwavering commitment to the defense of Japan under our mutual security treaty, which covers the Senkaku Islands. As India is the world's largest democracy and a Major Defense Partner, the United States and India will work together, bilaterally and multilaterally, to support our shared vision of a free and open Indo-Pacific. We will seek sustained diplomacy with North Korea to make tangible progress toward the complete denuclearization of the Korean Peninsula, while strengthening extended deterrence in the face of North Korean weapons of mass destruction and missile threats. The brutal military coup in Burma has undermined regional stability, and we will continue working closely with allies and partners, including ASEAN, to help restore Burma's democratic transition.

We will also work to enhance partners' resilience to transnational challenges, including climate and biological threats. The Indo-Pacific is the epicenter of the climate crisis but is also essential to climate solutions, and our shared responses to the climate crisis are a political imperative and an economic opportunity. We are also partnering to help the region build resilience to pandemic disease and to strengthen their health systems, drive investments in global health security, and expand the region's ability to prevent, detect, and respond to emergencies.

We have entered a consequential new period of American foreign policy that will demand more of the United States in the Indo-Pacific than has been asked of us since the Second World War. No region will be of more significance to the world and to everyday Americans than the Indo-Pacific. We are ambitious because we know that we and our allies and partners hold a common vision for its future.

Deepen Our Alliance with Europe

With a relationship rooted in shared democratic values, common interests, and historic ties, the transatlantic relationship is a vital platform on which many other elements of our foreign policy are built. Europe has been, and will continue to be, our foundational partner in addressing the full range of global challenges. To effectively pursue a common global agenda, we are broadening and deepening the transatlantic bond—strengthening NATO, raising the level of ambition in the U.S.-EU relationship, and standing with our European allies and partners in defense of the rules-based system that underpins our security, prosperity, and values.

Today, Europe stands at the front lines of the fight to defend the principles of freedom, sovereignty, and non-aggression, and we will continue to work in lockstep to ensure that freedom prevails. America remains unequivocally committed to collective defense as enshrined in NATO's Article 5 and will work alongside our NATO Allies to deter, defend against, and build resilience to aggression and coercion in all its forms. As we step up our own sizable

★ ★ ★ ★ ★

contributions to NATO capabilities and readiness—including by strengthening defensive forces and capabilities, and upholding our long-standing commitment to extended deterrence—we will count on our Allies to continue assuming greater responsibility by increasing their spending, capabilities, and contributions. European defense investments, through or complementary to NATO, will be critical to ensuring our shared security at this time of intensifying competition. We stand behind NATO's continued adaptation to modern security challenges, including its emphasis on defense in cyberspace, climate security, and the growing security risks presented by the PRC's policies and actions.

America maintains our fundamental commitment to the pursuit of a Europe that is whole, free, and at peace. Russia's further invasion of Ukraine poses a grave threat to this vision, which is why we are determined to support Ukraine in defending its sovereignty and territorial integrity while imposing severe costs on Moscow for its aggression. We have supported Ukraine with security, humanitarian, and financial assistance. We have joined with allies and partners in Europe and around the globe to impose sanctions and export controls that will degrade Russia's ability to wage future wars of aggression. We have partnered with the European Commission on an ambitious plan to reduce Europe's dependence on Russian fossil fuels, strengthen European energy security, and advance shared climate goals. Across these efforts, the EU—an integrated market of over 450 million people—is an indispensable partner, and we support efforts to foster EU unity. We also encourage close cooperation on matters of mutual interest between the EU and the United Kingdom. In addition, we underscore our support for the Good Friday Agreement which is the bedrock of peace, stability, and prosperity in Northern Ireland.

As we support Ukraine, we will also work to enhance the stability and resilience of other democracies. We will support the European aspirations of Georgia and Moldova and their commitment to important institutional reforms. We will assist partners in strengthening democratic institutions, the rule of law, and economic development in the Western Balkans. We will back diplomatic efforts to resolve conflict in the South Caucasus. We will continue to engage with Turkey to reinforce its strategic, political, economic, and institutional ties to the West. We will work with allies and partners to manage the refugee crisis created by Russia's war in Ukraine. And, we will work to forestall terrorist threats to Europe. Elsewhere in Eurasia, we will continue to support the independence, sovereignty and territorial integrity of Central Asia. We will foster efforts to enhance resilience and democratic development in the five countries in this region. We will continue to work through the C5+1 diplomatic platform (Kazakhstan, Kyrgyz Republic, Tajikistan, Turkmenistan, Uzbekistan and the United States) to advance climate adaptation, improve regional energy and food security, enhance integration within the region, and build greater connectivity to global markets.

Though rooted in transatlantic strength and stability, our agenda with European allies and partners is global. We will work with the EU to strengthen trade, investment, and technological cooperation grounded in shared democratic values—promoting an open and inclusive global economy, setting high standards for trade, ensuring fair competition, supporting labor rights, driving decarbonization, fighting corruption, and protecting our innovations from uses that run counter to our interests and values. Through the G7, we will work with France, Germany, Italy, and the United Kingdom to galvanize international cooperation on the world's most pressing challenges. We will jointly defend human rights, whether in Belarus or Xinjiang. To enact this ambitious agenda, we will deepen our strategic alignment—consulting regularly, sharing information and intelligence, and acting together.

★ ★ ★ ★ ★ ★

Foster Democracy and Shared Prosperity in the Western Hemisphere

No region impacts the United States more directly than the Western Hemisphere. With $1.9 trillion in annual trade, shared values and democratic traditions, and familial bonds, nations of the Western Hemisphere, especially in North America, are key contributors to U.S. prosperity and resilience. But the COVID-19 pandemic and ensuing recession have exacerbated longstanding structural challenges, fueled political and social unrest, undermining faith in democracy's ability to deliver, and spurred unprecedented levels of irregular migration to the United States and throughout the region. Recognizing the direct link between the region's prosperity and security and that of our own, it is vital for the United States to revitalize our partnerships to build and preserve economic resilience, democratic stability, and citizen security within the hemisphere. We will advance these efforts through regular interactions, multilateral and institutional collaboration, and regional initiatives, and by implementing the commitments made at the Ninth Summit of the Americas.

The movement of people throughout the Americas, including over six million Venezuelans forced to leave their homes since 2015, affects all of Latin America and the Caribbean and reinforces the need for regional action. The Los Angeles Declaration on Migration and Protection complements U.S. efforts at home to modernize its border infrastructure and build a fair, orderly, and humane immigration system with a bold hemisphere-wide partnership centered on the principle of responsibility-sharing, stability and assistance for affected communities, the expansion of legal pathways, humane migration management, and a coordinated emergency response. The United States is also leading the charge to expand legal pathways for migration and to combat illicit human smuggling and trafficking that prey on vulnerable migrants. These efforts combined aim to stabilize migrant populations and replace irregular migration with orderly flows that can fuel economic growth in the United States and across the region. We will pursue these collaborative efforts while ensuring a fundamentally fair, orderly, and humane approach to migration management that bolster border security and protects our nation.

Ending and mitigating the effects of the COVID-19 pandemic and advancing health security are imperative for the wellbeing of the entire hemisphere. In addition to donating over 72 million vaccines, through the Action Plan on Health and Resilience in the Americas we are partnering with the region to prevent, prepare for, and respond to future pandemic threats and other public health emergencies while also expanding the equitable delivery of healthcare and public services to remote, vulnerable, and marginalized populations. In addition to supporting countries, especially in Central America and the Caribbean, in reaching a 70 percent COVID-19 vaccination rate, associated partnerships are boosting increased vaccine manufacturing capability and helping train 500,000 public health and medical professionals by 2027 through the Americas Health Corps.

Together with regional partners we are deepening economic cooperation to ensure durable and inclusive economic growth that delivers for our working people. Our priority is to work with Canada and Mexico to advance a North American vision for the future that draws on our shared strengths and bolsters U.S. global competitiveness. Similarly, the Americas Partnership for Economic Prosperity will guide our regional economic engagement by focusing on the largest drivers of bottom-up and middle-out growth, updating tools for the new and complex challenges facing us today and in the decades to come with a focus on reinvigorating regional economic

★ ★ ★ ★ ★ ★

institutions, securing supply chains, creating clean energy jobs and promoting decarbonization, ensuring sustainable and inclusive trade, and making game-changing investments that increase the effectiveness of public administration.

Tackling the climate crisis and harnessing the dynamism of the region will be central to our approach, and we will use mitigation and adaptation efforts to fuel a sustainable economic recovery and protect forest ecosystems, including by promoting trade and investment in clean energy to achieve a collective target of 70 percent installed capacity for renewable energy generation in the region's electricity sector by 2030 and mobilizing financing and other forms of support to promote conservation of the Amazon. The United States and the Caribbean Community also launched the Partnership to Address the Climate Crisis 2030 to expand access to project financing, attract private investment in clean energy infrastructure and climate adaptation projects, and enhance local capacity to assess, plan for, predict, mitigate, and respond to extreme weather events and related risks in a changing climate.

The United States derives security and economic benefits from the region's democratic stability and institutions, as our shared values provide a basis for collaboration and peaceful dispute resolution. To help preserve and enhance these traditions, we will support partners striving to build transparent, inclusive, and accountable institutions. Together, we will support effective democratic governance responsive to citizen needs, defend human rights and combat gender-based violence, tackle corruption, and protect against external interference or coercion, including from the PRC, Russia, or Iran. Through reinvigorated and representative Inter-American institutions, and in partnership with civil society and other governments, we will support democratic self-determination for the people of Venezuela, Cuba, Nicaragua, and any country where the popular will is suppressed. In Haiti, which suffers from an extended humanitarian, political, and economic crisis, we will mobilize the international community to help restore security, rebuild governing institutions, and support a foundation of prosperity by which the Haitian people can determine their own future.

We will also assist partners in facing security threats. These challenges may be internal—including from local gangs, or transnational, including from criminal organizations that traffic drugs and humans and undertake other illegal operations—or external, as malign actors seek to gain military or intelligence footholds in the region. These threats impact security throughout the Americas, including here at home, and we will therefore promote collaboration to help assist civilian police and, strengthen justice systems in the Americas, and expand information sharing with our partners.

These priorities—expanding economic opportunities, strengthening democracy, and building security—are mutually reinforcing and contribute to national, regional, and global stability. We have an overriding strategic interest in pursuing and strengthening collaboration through intensified diplomatic engagement with hemispheric partners and institutions based on the premise that advance a vision of a region that is secure, middle class, and democratic is fundamentally in the national security interest of the United States. The challenge and the stakes of this undertaking are accentuated by the backdrop of increased geopolitical and geoeconomics volatility, the interrelated challenges posed by phenomena like climate change, global pandemics, and mass migration, and the recognition that the security and prosperity of the United States hinges on that of our neighbors.

★ ★ ★ ★ ★ ★

Support De-Escalation and Integration in the Middle East

Over the past two decades, U.S. foreign policy has focused predominantly on threats emanating from the Middle East and North Africa. We have too often defaulted to military-centric policies underpinned by an unrealistic faith in force and regime change to deliver sustainable outcomes, while failing to adequately account for opportunity costs to competing global priorities or unintended consequences. It is time to eschew grand designs in favor of more practical steps that can advance U.S. interests and help regional partners lay the foundation for greater stability, prosperity, and opportunity for the people of the Middle East and for the American people.

The United States has set forth a new framework for U.S. policy in the region based on America's unparalleled comparative advantage in building partnerships, coalitions, and alliances to strengthen deterrence, while using diplomacy to de-escalate tensions, reduce risks of new conflicts, and set a long-term foundation for stability.

This framework has five principles. First, the United States will support and strengthen partnerships with countries that subscribe to the rules-based international order, and we will make sure those countries can defend themselves against foreign threats. Second, the United States will not allow foreign or regional powers to jeopardize freedom of navigation through the Middle East's waterways, including the Strait of Hormuz and the Bab al Mandab, nor tolerate efforts by any country to dominate another—or the region—through military buildups, incursions, or threats. Third, even as the United States works to deter threats to regional stability, we will work to reduce tensions, de-escalate, and end conflicts wherever possible through diplomacy. Fourth, the United States will promote regional integration by building political, economic, and security connections between and among U.S. partners, including through integrated air and maritime defense structures, while respecting each country's sovereignty and independent choices. Fifth, the United States will always promote human rights and the values enshrined in the UN Charter.

This new framework builds on the recent progress regional states have made to bridge their enduring divides. We will continue to work with allies and partners to enhance their capabilities to deter and counter Iran's destabilizing activities. We will pursue diplomacy to ensure that Iran can never acquire a nuclear weapon, while remaining postured and prepared to use other means should diplomacy fail. Iran's threats against U.S. personnel as well as current and former U.S. officials will not be tolerated, and as we have demonstrated, we will respond when our people and interests are attacked. As we do so, we will always stand with the Iranian people striving for the basic rights and dignity long denied them by the regime in Tehran.

More broadly we will combine diplomacy, economic aid, and security assistance to local partners to alleviate suffering, reduce instability, and prevent the export of terrorism or mass migration from Yemen, Syria, and Libya, while working with regional governments to manage the broader impact of these challenges. We will seek to extend and deepen Israel's growing ties to its neighbors and other Arab states, including through the Abraham Accords, while maintaining our ironclad commitment to its security. We will also continue to promote a viable two state solution that preserves Israel's future as a Jewish and democratic state while meeting Palestinian aspirations for a secure and viable state of their own. As President Biden stated during his visit to the West Bank in July 2022, "Two States along the 1967 lines, with mutually agreed swaps, remain the best way to achieve equal measure of security, prosperity, freedom, and democracy for Palestinians as well as Israelis."

This new framework relies on a sustainable and effective military posture focused on deterrence, strengthening partner capacity, enabling regional security integration, countering terrorist threats, and ensuring the free flow of global commerce. In conjunction with the use of other instruments of national power, these military activities also help counter external actors' military expansion in the region. We will not use our military to change regimes or remake societies, but instead limit the use of force to circumstances where it is necessary to protect our national security interests and consistent with international law, while enabling our partners to defend their territory from external and terrorist threats.

We will encourage economic and political reforms that help unlock the region's potential, including by fostering greater economic integration to drive growth and create jobs. We will encourage energy producers to use their resources to stabilize global energy markets, while also preparing for a clean energy future and protecting American consumers. We will also continue to support our democratic partners and demand accountability for violations of human rights, recognizing that while true reform can only come from within, the United States still has an important role to play. The United States is the largest bilateral donor of humanitarian assistance and a longstanding champion for principled, needs-based humanitarian action. We will sustain our leadership on humanitarian assistance and manage long-term refugee and displacement crises, which help realize human dignity and bolster stability. And we will accelerate our support to regional partners to help them build greater resilience, as the future of the Middle East will be defined as much by climate, technological, and demographic changes as by traditional security matters.

Build 21st Century U.S.-Africa Partnerships

Africa's governments, institutions, and people are a major geopolitical force, one that will play a crucial role in solving global challenges in the coming decade. Africa is more youthful, mobile, educated, and connected than ever before. African countries comprise one of the largest regional voting groups at the UN and their citizens lead major international institutions. The continent's booming population, vital natural resources, and vibrant entrepreneurship, coupled with the African Continental Free Trade Area, have the potential to drive transformative economic growth. Our partnerships with African states over the past three decades helped lay the groundwork for this growth. To accelerate it, U.S.-Africa partnerships must adapt to reflect the important geopolitical role that African nations play globally.

Advancing America's national interests will hinge in part on working more closely, not only with African nations, but also with regional bodies, such as the African Union, subnational governments, civil society, and private sector and diaspora communities. We will continue to invest in the region's largest states, such as Nigeria, Kenya, and South Africa, while also deepening our ties to medium and small states. We will engage African countries as equal partners to achieve our shared priorities from health and pandemic preparedness to climate change. We will also press partners about human rights, corruption, or authoritarian behavior, and deepen partnerships with countries that make progress toward more open and democratic governance. In coordination with international partners and regional bodies, we will counter democratic backsliding by imposing costs for coups and pressing for progress on civilian transitions. And we will listen to African leaders and people as they articulate their vision for their foreign partnerships, including expectations for transparency, accountability, fairness, inclusion, and equity.

Enhancing Africa's peace and prosperity will bolster Africa's ability to solve regional and global problems. The region's commitment and capacity to renew democracy, as well as anticipate, prevent, and address emerging and long running conflicts can lead to favorable outcomes for Africans and Americans. We will support African-led efforts to work toward political solutions to costly conflicts, increasing terrorist activity, and humanitarian crises, such as those in Cameroon, Democratic Republic of the Congo, Ethiopia, Mozambique, Nigeria, Somalia, and the Sahel, and invest in local and international peacebuilding and peacekeeping to prevent new conflicts from emerging. Consistent with our broader counterterrorism approach, we will disrupt and degrade terrorist threats against the United States while supporting partners to prevent terrorist expansion. We will work with our African and international partners to tackle the root causes of terrorism, including by countering corruption, strengthening accountability and justice, investing in inclusive economic development, and advancing human rights, including women's rights, and also push back on the destabilizing impact of the Russia-backed Wagner Group.

We will support accelerating growth through private sector investment, help Africa unlock its digital economy, double down on tackling food insecurity, and expand clean energy infrastructure through the Prosper Africa, Feed the Future, and Power Africa initiatives. We will support climate adaptation, conservation, and a just energy transition, as sub-Saharan African countries are already experiencing severe climate impacts, compounding land use, migration challenges, and rising food and commodity prices, made worse by Russia's further invasion of Ukraine. Quality healthcare systems are essential to economic growth, and we will build on our decades-long partnerships to invest in health security and health systems infrastructure, and the ongoing COVID-19 response. We will also work with African governments to create the business environments and make the investments in human capital and capacity development to attract investors, grow businesses, and create good jobs across sectors—and to bolster U.S.-Africa trade and create new opportunities for U.S. businesses. We will seek to offer opportunities that reflect America's competitive advantages, promoting inclusive growth, respecting workers' rights, and protecting the region's resources for future generations.

Maintain a Peaceful Arctic

The United States seeks an Arctic region that is peaceful, stable, prosperous, and cooperative. Climate change is making the Arctic more accessible than ever, threatening Arctic communities and vital ecosystems, creating new potential economic opportunities. and intensifying competition to shape the region's future. Russia has invested significantly in its presence in the Arctic over the last decade, modernizing its military infrastructure and increasing the pace of exercises and training operations. Its aggressive behavior has raised geopolitical tensions in the Arctic, creating new risks of unintended conflict and hindering cooperation. The PRC has also sought to increase its influence in the Arctic by rapidly increased its Arctic investments, pursuing new scientific activities, and using these scientific engagements to conduct dual-use research with intelligence or military applications.

We will uphold U.S. security in the region by improving our maritime domain awareness, communications, disaster response capabilities, and icebreaking capacity to prepare for increased international activity in the region. We will exercise U.S. Government presence in the region as

★ ★ ★ ★ ★ ★

required, while reducing risk and preventing unnecessary escalation. Arctic nations have the primary responsibility for addressing regional challenges, and we will deepen our cooperation with our Arctic allies and partners and work with them to sustain the Arctic Council and other Arctic institutions despite the challenges to Arctic cooperation posed by Russia's war in Ukraine. We will continue to protect freedom of navigation and determine the U.S. extended continental shelf in accordance with international rules. We must build resilience to and mitigate climate change in the region, including through agreements to reduce emissions and more cross-Arctic research collaboration. As economic activity in the Arctic increases, we will invest in infrastructure, improve livelihoods, and encourage responsible private sector investment by the United States, our allies, and our partners, including in critical minerals, and improve investment screening for national security purposes. Across these efforts, we will uphold our commitment to honor Tribal sovereignty and self-governance through regular, meaningful, and robust consultation and collaboration with Alaska Native communities.

Protect Sea, Air, and Space

People around the world depend on the sea, air, and space for their security and prosperity. The world's interconnected oceans, lands, waterways, and other ecosystems generate economic opportunity and enable critical commercial and military activity. They contain biodiversity vital to food security, clean air and water, a stable climate, and health and wellbeing. Threats to these systems—including excessive maritime and airspace claims, pollution and unregulated deforestation, and wildlife trafficking and illegal, unreported, and unregulated fishing—impact governments' abilities to meet basic human needs and contribute to political, economic, and social instability. We will stand up for freedom of navigation and overflight, support environmental protection, and oppose destructive distant water fishing practices by upholding international laws and norms, including the customary international law rules in the UN Convention on the Law of the Sea. And we will promote Antarctica's status as a continent reserved for peace and science in accordance with the provisions of the Antarctic Treaty of 1959.

Space exploration and use benefits humanity, from creating economic opportunities to developing new technologies and enabling climate surveillance. America will maintain our position as the world's leader in space and work alongside the international community to ensure the domain's sustainability, safety, stability, and security. We must lead in updating outer space governance, establishing a space traffic coordination system and charting a path for future space norms and arms control. Working with allies and partners, we will develop policies and regulations that enable the burgeoning U.S. commercial space sector to compete internationally. We will enhance the resilience of U.S. space systems that we rely on for critical national and homeland security functions. These efforts aim to protect U.S. interests in space, avoid destabilizing arms races, and responsibly steward the space environment.

★ ★ ★ ★ ★ ★

Sharpen Our Tools of Statecraft

Our national security institutions and workforce underpin America's global leadership and the security, prosperity, and freedoms of the American people. To achieve our ambitious aims, we must modernize and adapt our tools of statecraft for today's challenges. For example, we are:

- Strengthening American diplomacy by modernizing the Department of State, including through the recent creation of a new bureau for cyberspace and digital policy and special envoy for critical and emerging technologies.
- Adapting the Intelligence Community (IC), including by aligning our organizations to better address competition, embracing new data tools, and enhancing integration of open source material.
- Enhancing U.S. and global early warning and forecasting for infectious disease threats and pandemics by increasing support for the Centers for Disease Control and Prevention's (CDC) Center for Outbreak, Forecasting, and Analytics and foreign assistance for global health security.
- Reorganizing the Office of the Under Secretary of Defense for Policy to sharpen its focus on emerging technologies and elevate senior leader attention to critical regions. Bolstering the Department of Homeland Security's (DHS) Cybersecurity Service by reimagining how DHS hires, develops, and retains top-tier and diverse cyber talent.
- Making development assistance more accessible and equitable by increasing engagement with and shifting 25 percent of U.S. Agency for International Development (USAID) funding to local partners, and double USAID's work on empowering women and girls.
- Expanding our engagement with stakeholders and build our capacity to partner with the private sector, philanthropy, diaspora communities, and civil society.
- Prioritizing technology's role in national security by elevating the White House Office of Science and Technology Policy to a cabinet-level agency and full member of the National Security Council.

The success of these efforts and our foreign policy will require strengthening the national security workforce by recruiting and retaining diverse, high-caliber talent. We are:

- Prioritizing diversity, equity, inclusion, and accessibility to ensure national security institutions reflect the American public they represent.
- Creating more effective and efficient hiring, recruitment, retention, and talent development practices, particularly in STEM fields, economics, critical languages, and regional affairs.
- Supporting professional development opportunities—for both leadership and technical skills—at all levels of the workforce.
- Opening opportunities for the national security workforce to move among institutions, both within and outside government, and carry the skills they develop back to their home agencies.
- Equipping the workforce with cutting-edge technology and better integrate data and analytic tools to support decision-making.
- Prioritizing human resources capabilities and personnel, who will drive and steward all of these initiatives.

★ ★ ★ ★ ★ ★

The health of our national security institutions and workforce relies on faith in the apolitical nature of Federal law enforcement agencies, the IC, our diplomats, civil servants, Federally funded research and development institutions, and military as we work together in national service.

PART V: CONCLUSION

We are confident that the United States, alongside our allies and partners, is positioned to succeed in our pursuit of a free, open, prosperous, and secure global order. With the key elements outlined in this strategy, we will tackle the twin challenges of our time: out-competing our rivals to shape the international order while tackling shared challenges, including climate change, pandemic preparedness, and food security, that will define the next stage of human history. We will strengthen democracy across the world, and multilateral institutions, as we look to the future to chart new and fair rules of the road for emerging technology, cybersecurity, and trade and economics. And we will do all this and more by leveraging our considerable advantages and our unparalleled coalition of allies and partners.

As we implement this strategy, we will continually assess and reassess our approach to ensure we are best serving the American people. We will be guided by the indisputable fact that the strength and quality of the American project at home is inextricably linked with our leadership in the world and our ability to shape the terms of the world order. This National Security Strategy will be evaluated by an overriding metric: whether it makes life better, safer, and fairer for the people of the United States, and whether it lifts up the countries and people around the world who share our vision for the future.

We are motivated by a clear vision of what success looks like at the end of this decisive decade.

By enhancing our industrial capacity, investing in our people, and strengthening our democracy, we will have strengthened the foundation of our economy, bolstered our national resilience, enhanced our credibility on the world stage, and ensured our competitive advantages.

By deepening and expanding our diplomatic relationships not only with our democratic allies but with all states who share our vision for a better future, we will have developed terms of competition with our strategic rivals that are favorable to our interests and values and laid the foundation to increase cooperation on shared challenges.

By modernizing our military, pursuing advanced technologies, and investing in our defense workforce, we will have strengthened deterrence in an era of increasing geopolitical confrontation, and positioned America to defend our homeland, our allies, partners, and interests overseas, and our values across the globe.

By leveraging our national strengths and rallying a broad coalition of allies and partners, we will advance our vision of a free, open, prosperous, and secure world, outmaneuvering our competitors, and making meaningful progress on issues like climate change, global health, and food security to improve the lives not just of Americans but of people around the world.

This is what we must achieve in this decisive decade. As we have done throughout our history, America will seize this moment and rise to the challenge. There is no time to waste.

*9 781608 882434 *